I0094996

Africa and Europe: a Shared Future

PETER LANG

Bruxelles · Bern · Berlin · New York · Oxford · Wien

Alberto Majocchi (ed.)

Africa and Europe: a Shared Future

This book was made possible by the Centro Studi sul Federalismo (www.csfederalismo.it).

CENTRO STUDI SUL FEDERALISMO

This publication has been peer reviewed.

No part of this book may be reproduced in any form, by print, photocopy, microfilm or any other means, without prior written permission from the publisher. All rights reserved.

© P.I.E. PETER LANG s.a.
International Academic Publishers
Brussels, 2020
1 avenue Maurice, B-1050 Brussels, Belgium
brussels@peterlang.com; www.peterlang.com

ISSN 2294-6969
ISBN 978-2-8076-1555-7
ePDF 978-2-8076-1556-4
ePUB 978-2-8076-1557-1
MOBI 978-2-8076-1558-8
DOI 10.3726/b16969
D/2020/5678/24

Bibliographic information published by "Die Deutsche Nationalbibliothek".

"Die Deutsche National Bibliothek" lists this publication in the "Deutsche Nationalbibliografie"; detailed bibliographic data is available on the Internet at <http://dnb.de>.

TABLE OF CONTENTS

Foreword

ROMANO PRODI

The analysis offered in this collection of essays does not focus on Africa's tragedies and challenges; rather it outlines a possible strategy for its future. This approach is what makes this short book original and its analysis distinctive. Of all the changes in the African scenario, with respect to the rest of the world, this book focusses on Africa's political, institutional and economic characteristics in order to point out its opportunities. There is no complaint or despair in it; this series of essays by different authors offers instead a lucid, realistic analysis of the future possibilities of the African continent.

The first challenge concerns Africa's opportunity to exploit its great potential, which would truly make it a continent whose unity, while certainly based on its sub-regional dimensions, is however capable of expressing a common strategy. In order to do this its sub-regional dimensions must be strengthened, but without neglecting the creation of a network between them. This is no easy task because it requires intense institutional work. Agreements aimed at creating a single market for the entire African continent have now taken a big step forward in this direction. These agreements – totally impossible until a few years ago – have in fact led to the Treaty establishing the African Continental Free Trade Area (AfCTA), which entered into force in 2019. However, this important result is clearly not enough: in fact, there cannot be an African market without building the infrastructure necessary for free trade.

Institutional progress must not be underestimated since it is an essential, indispensable prerequisite both for the creation of sufficiently large markets and for the development of economies of scale that will allow Africa to become a leading player, not only in the trade of raw materials, as is already the case now, but also in manufactured goods and agricultural products.

This analysis then stresses the responsibility and role played by the European Union toward Africa, not only with regard to economics and politics, but also to the major problem of emigration. This problem does not impact on China, the other major player in economic relations with Africa: therefore this creates large imbalances when it comes to Europe's responsibilities in relations with Africa. Against the background of the role and great synergies between China and Africa, it is right for this volume to address the need for a new alliance between Europe and China. On the other hand, hardly any reference is made to the United States, whose interest in Africa is almost exclusively part of its global and military strategy. The fact that the US is self-sufficient in energy has a surplus in agricultural production and that raw materials are widely available indeed make the relationship between the United States and Africa much more tenuous than the relationship between Africa and Europe or between Africa and China. In fact, unlike the United States, China needs to import raw materials, agricultural products and energy, not only for its development, but also for its own subsistence.

As regards relations between Africa and Europe and between Africa and China, this volume then addresses the great challenge of employment. While it is clear that building infrastructure is in fact necessary for job creation, it is also true that this is not enough.

Another very interesting issue regards the sought-after and very important economic and political relationship between Africa and Europe. It is of great interest to explore how this can be strengthened through a broad agreement to provide electricity for the indispensable economic life of the continent. In fact, not only do 300 million Africans not have access to clean water, but also more than twice as many have no access to electricity, without which there can be neither agriculture nor industry. Hence, one obvious solution is to come up with proposals and projects dedicated to creating great prospects for energy production from renewables, such as wind and mainly solar energy – potentially abundant throughout the African continent. However, triggering what we might call the "renewable energy revolution" in Africa requires a sound political strategy: strong synergies with Europe and a close relationship with Africa within a regulatory framework that, once again, expresses continental unity to the greatest extent possible. It is also clear that energy is an ideal area where China and Europe could collaborate on a major project. In theory, this could be crucial to finally implementing the Silk Road. It is equally true that there is no point in hiding the political difficulties that stand in the way of this obvious and convenient source of cooperation.

This interesting and refined synthesis on Africa offers more than just negative perspectives; it certainly shifts away from the difficult and complex reality in which Africa finds itself in order to pave the way to a possible development perspective that seems to be an opportunity that cannot be missed.

Introduction

ALBERTO MAJOCCHI

After the end of the Cold War, the interest of the superpowers in the African continent progressively weakened, and the role of Africa in world politics has become marginalized. But, recently, this trend has been substantially reversed for two co-evolving reasons: on the one hand, Africa's rich supply of raw materials and agricultural products, which has attracted above all the interest of China and, on the other hand, the problem of migration, which has directly impacted European countries and highlighted an urgent need to support the development of the African continent.

In recent decades, Africa has made significant progress on several fronts. At the political level, democracy has been strengthened, with the generalization of electoral processes and greater political stability. At the same time, the process of progressive integration at the continental level has been consolidated with the emergence of the African Union as a reference point for the politics of African countries on economic and security issues. On an economic level, growth rates have been quite high, albeit uneven between different states, and recently the process for the creation of an African Continental Free Trade Area has started, which represents a pre-requisite for kick-starting endogenous growth in the African economy. But, despite these improvements, living conditions are still difficult and push ever larger masses to move toward Europe to secure a better future. And this push is also sustained by conditions of insecurity and serious violations of human rights in some areas of the continent.

In Europe, the financial crisis highlighted the limits of the construction of the economic and monetary union, due to the difficulty of combining monetary policy with fiscal policy interventions, in particular to support an active investment policy and to reduce inequalities both at the territorial level and within member countries. During the crisis, numerous interventions were made to prevent dramatic developments. On the one hand, with the Fiscal Compact, the constraints on national budget policies were strengthened to avoid the negative external effects of excessive deficits of the weakest countries, while, with the creation of the European Stability Mechanism, a support to financial stability was guaranteed, promoted above all through Quantitative Easing, implemented by the European Central Bank. On the other hand, with the launch of the Juncker Plan, the foundations were laid for an innovative policy to support investments, thanks to a guarantee mechanism that promotes and supports private investments in the market.

With the economic recovery, and in view of the approval of the Multiannual Financial Framework 2021–2027, the fundamental theme for the European Union concerns the availability of adequate resources to finance policies that appear indispensable to guaranteeing a future of sustainable growth for Europe. In the first place, it is a question of guaranteeing internal and external security, in a world in which the American guarantee for European security has vanished; to manage the problem of migratory flows with the financing of the 'Growth Plan with Africa', managed in agreement with the African Union; to guarantee resources to stabilize the European economy in the face of general or asymmetric shocks that may affect it in the future; to promote research and technological development, including the creation of European champions in the leading technological sectors; and, finally, to finance a *Social Green New Deal*, which will move Europe along a path of sustainable development from the environmental, economic and social points of view, allowing inequalities, deepened during the crisis and as a result of globalization processes, to be overcome.

In this context, there is a major issue that has aroused in Europe a strong interest in African development, and it is the problem of climate change, that is predominantly linked to the consumption of fossil fuel. Europe is committed to strongly reduce its fossil fuel needs in the coming decades, to achieve by 2050 carbon neutrality, thus complying with the commitments of the Paris Agreement of 2015. But this reduction must be accompanied by a growth in renewable energy availability, and Africa is a potential source of green energy supply. However, this availability can only become effective with major investment and new infrastructure. A *Growth Plan with Africa* will have to be carried out, in full cooperation between the European Union and the African Union, and may represent the pivotal point of an ecological transition that will launch the two continents in the direction of sustainable development.

The Center for Studies on Federalism has, for a number of years, been reflecting on the relations between Europe and Africa regarding political, economic and security issues. In this book, we have collected a series of studies by researchers linked to the Center, which address the different aspects of these relationships, to support a debate that will lead to decisions that will be crucial for the future of both Continents. First of all, the theme of the new role of Africa in the world equilibrium is tackled, following the end of bipolarism and the growth of globalization. We examine the process of integration of African countries from a historical point of view, considering in particular the comparison between pan-Africanist and regionalist tendencies, while in the economic perspective, the accent is placed on recent developments linked to the historic decision to create an African free trade area. The growth of the economy of African countries in recent decades is significant, but not sufficient to guarantee an increase in the standard of living of the population capable of guaranteeing, in the medium-long term, a brake on the migration processes that drain the best resources of the continent: human capital. European plans to support the development of African countries are evaluated for their immediate effects and in the longer-term prospects. Finally, the prospect of the creation of a common currency – or of a unit of account – to be used in inter-African payments is analyzed; this offers the chance to both break the dependence on other currencies and the disparities between different currency areas, still linked to the old colonial borders.

The contributions collected in this volume, though addressed with different methodologies, are however linked by a common thread: the development of Africa is a problem that must be faced and solved by the peoples of the continent, with the aim of consolidating democracy and fragile institutional structures and of guaranteeing a future of growth and progressive improvement in the quality of life. However, Europe has a role and a responsibility in this process: firstly, after having imposed on Africa the model of the bureaucratic and centralized national state, Europe today can represent a model of integration, on the economic field and, in prospect, on the political terrain. Beyond this, Europe must offer a partnership relationship with Africa to start a Green New Deal for Europe and Africa together, not only with the allocation of financial resources, but also technology transfers and infrastructure creation. But, in this partnership for growth, the initiative must be entrusted to

African countries, as was the case for Europe in the case of the Marshall Plan: Europe's sole permitted condition must be that their plan be drawn up in common and placed in the perspective of strengthening the process of economic and political integration already started on the Continent. The growth of democracy and the protection of human rights in the countries of the Continent could be enhanced if the African Union was linked to the working of the Council of Europe, as it is the case for Tunisia and Morocco, and could obtain the status of observer that has already been granted in the past to the Vatican City State. Ultimately, the partnership between Europe and Africa can represent an emblematic case of win-win policy, and in this partnership, the greatest responsibility lies with Europe that must complete its own unification process to be endowed with the political capability to guarantee Africa's future of growth in stability and security.

Africa in a Changing International Scenario

Paolo Sannella

1. From the Beginning: A Long Journey

Today it is still difficult to talk about Africa and Africans without arguments, judgments and preconceptions getting in the way.

There is no doubt that the immense area south of the Sahara long remained foreign to European history, the long dominant world history. Protected to the north by the almost insurmountable frontier of that immense desert, African societies had for centuries escaped contact with the populations to the north, to which they probably provided the first vital impulse through the original transmigration of nuclei of original hominids from its eastern regions and the valleys of today's Kenya. In this vast "island" south of the Sahara, black men, mostly grouped in small villages scattered over large areas, lived their history far from us, building their more or less large and efficient political and administrative organizations. They developed their cultures and the many different interpretations of themselves and nature. However, they undeniably fell behind in technology, partly due to their specific geographical and climatic conditions and partly to the relative fragmentation of the micro-communities residing in that territory and their isolation from the rest of the world. This greatly facilitated the arrival and penetration of the first groups and the first cultural expressions of the outside world.

A few centuries ago, in fact, when substantial elements of the "other" world arrived in Africa, not only from Europe but also from the Arabian Peninsula and the East, African society showed its mainly technological fragility. This fragility was also the result of fundamental structural problems: the dispersion of its scarce population over immense, inhospitable territories associated with the lack of common and widely practiced writing and languages.

The image of an underdeveloped Africa and of Africans as peoples needing to be educated, redeemed and civilized thus took root in European culture and through it in world consciousness. Until a few decades ago, this was the Africa we knew, in addition to being a continent full of wonderful natural beauty and variety. The Catholic Church also reminded us that black men had no soul and were therefore hardly comparable to other men. This prevailing interpretation, strongly supported by economic and strategic interests, justified colonial domination, the use of and trade in slaves, the enslavement of men and peoples, the systematic destruction of cultures, and civil and religious institutions. It can be said with certainty that, with very few exceptions, this was Africa's position on the world stage and in the collective consciousness until very recently: just a few decades ago. Even today, when the son of a black African rises to the presidency of the most powerful world empire governed by whites, it is surprising to see how this "position" of Africa often continues to emerge and hinder the interpretation of the present.

In a crescendo of increasingly dramatic, high-impact events, the last century actually saw a radical change in the situation in Africa, which is now emerging with ever greater force onto the world stage, from which – unlike China and India – it had always been distant. Returning to the focus of our discussion, it may be argued that although Africa has long been absent from the world stage, today it is making its presence known and perhaps preparing to become one of its central actors.

In my opinion, there is no doubt that the historical turning point took place in the 1960s, when, in quick succession, almost all the African states achieved independence. Their liberation took on different forms; however, this always – and for everyone – meant starting down the difficult path of creating nations and autonomous states to replace the old administrations. The black continent was no longer a passive player in history, an arena for the clash of European rivalries, with territories to be conquered and divvied up, according to their resources, to support the development of Europe and its economic and social revolution. The link between Capitalism, Colonialism and Imperialism that characterized Western history over the last two centuries may be constructed and deconstructed around Africa, its wealth, and its human and material resources. Its independence in the 1960s is the watershed which gave rise to a new Africa, the one we know today, that strangely seems to have little in common with Africa as it was and as we knew it; however, this feeling will disappear over the coming years as Africa takes her place on the world stage.

2. First Signs from the New World

In August this year, *New York Times Magazine* published a maxi-inquiry of great historical, political and social significance. Under this initiative – named *the 1619 Project* after the date when 400 years ago the African slave trade began and lasted until 1875 – the *New York Times* did not just want to entrust specialists with reinterpreting the slave trade in its historical, human and ethical terms; it wanted to try and further explore the impact of Africans' forced servitude on the foundation of the United States, first as an emerging power and then as a great world power. Regardless of whether they were located in the south or north and whether they were used for agricultural or industrial works or services, the research concluded by stressing how this cheap workforce, this transfusion of young, courageous and totally obedient energies, contributed greatly to the rapid accumulation of wealth and subsequent developments of that society. A similar phenomenon occurred, thanks to the use of the younger descendants of immigrant slaves in the armed forces.

This impressive new and different writing of U.S. history has provoked disappointment and criticism in certain areas of U.S. public opinion and scientific circles. However, it is still crucial to connect the two continents and acknowledge Africa's role as the driving force behind the U.S.'s power and global success. It is interesting to note that it is only possible to publicly state this now, even though this building on the past has been well known for a long time, because under Barack Obama's presidency, Africa and the Africans started to be recognized as equal and fundamental partners.

In September three years ago (20 September 2016), the CICOPS (Centre for International Cooperation and Development of the University of Pavia) held a conference entitled *An African Future for Europe* as part of a week dedicated to the study of the new dimensions of the international migration phenomenon, which aimed to challenge dominant thinking on Euro-African relations and act as a model for a possible different future configuration of those relationships. I feel moved when I recall Professor Calchi Novati's speech on that occasion, in what was one of his last public appearances. He recalled with accuracy and erudition the long history of European domination over the African continent, focusing in particular on the various attempts made by local societies to oppose – or at least to mitigate and moderate – that long European "present" imposed on Africa by the technological, military and political superiority of European states. In his conclusions, he also addressed the most pressing issue of modern development cooperation, recalling that even its most advanced forms – that sought to be credited as egalitarian and participatory – almost always concealed this same element of domination which in any case seems to characterize the relationship between those who "have" and those who "have not", or between those who "have more" and those who "have less", between those who offer and those who receive. He thought that no African development could change this state of affairs. This seemed to be his speech's bitter conclusion. Therefore, no significant "African Future for Europe", no fundamental change in power relations that for a long time to come would be presented as relations of cultural and political domination as well as economic exploitation.

I agreed not only with his impeccable historical reconstruction but also with his critical analysis of "cooperation" that appears increasingly distant from "development", and that only pays lip service to being a "partnership". What is more, at the time I thought – and even more so today – I could see in Africa's economic, political and cultural, but especially demographic, evolution those overwhelming new realities that would soon turn into the crucial factors of a new world order where Africa would also have the right to exist and to speak.

3. Africa on Its Way

Three years later, those new realities have been strengthened and confirmed again and again. Even in Italy, where events in Africa are traditionally followed with little interest, every day there have been initiatives that reflect this change. Month after month, the popular magazine *Africa e Affari* reports the data, characteristics and trends in these developments – especially in the economic field. These developments are starting to have a cumulative effect and an ever-greater impact on life and on the very structure of those societies, and then, inevitably, on international relations. It is almost pointless to recall that for over a decade the continent's economy as a whole has grown at an average rate of between 4 % and 5 % a year, and in some countries with double-digit

Asian-like rates, despite the world economic crisis in the same period. This is accompanied by a growth in a middle class with new economic and cultural interests, which, among other things, fosters the development of education, teaching and training systems as well as the emergence of new – domestic and international – players determined to participate in the development processes while offering valid dialogue and cooperation alternatives to local institutions and to those societies. Urban centers are developing due to a growing exodus from rural areas. Basic infrastructure is growing: with roads, railways, ports, airports and communication networks. Quality public and private training and research centers are being created – at university and in specializations. Finally, in many countries, the conditions of public "governance" are improving according to models very similar to those adopted on an international scale, without disregarding local needs and cultures. In terms of governmental capacity, Africa seems to be increasingly successful, for instance, in finding original solutions to the fundamental problem of creating nation-states beyond historico-cultural ethnic divisions, or in showing an increasingly widespread ability to manage the political transition and government changes in a satisfactory and peaceful way.

One of the most significant recent changes in this revolution that is shaking up Africa is the creation of the African Continental Free Trade Area (AfCFTA) last July in Niamey, with the initial accession of 22 states accounting for more than 1bn citizens. This is the largest free trade area in the world and will be a driving force for the continent toward the new and more significant goals of economic development and political cooperation.

All states around the world – not only the colonial or European states, as was the case just a few years ago – are looking at this new Africa with increasing interest. According to data summarized in a recent *Economist* study, 320 new embassies were opened between 2010 and 2016: the biggest "boom" in diplomatic construction in history! Turkey alone has opened 26 new embassies and India 18. This growing political and diplomatic attention goes hand in hand with the increased "weight" of the continent's countries. We would perhaps be equally surprised if we looked at the number of universities in Africa today compared to only half a century ago, or considered the overwhelming cultural developments such as the increased quality and quantity of African cinema or literature, not to mention the dominant role of African music or its sports champions, especially in some disciplines such as football and athletics.

4. Population Growth

This revolution in the economy, culture and politics goes hand in hand with what is truly the main agent of change in those societies: unparalleled demographic growth that has led the continent toward new domestic and international scenarios. Africa, which only half a century ago was less populated than Europe, today has twice as many inhabitants and is about to compete with Asia as the most populated continent: from 300-350m a few decades ago, to 1.2–1.3bn today, and perhaps 2.5bn in the very near future. All this has occurred – in some ways surprisingly – in a political and cultural climate characterized by the total lack of national and international policies to deal with the phenomenon. In fact, the population is growing despite decreasing birth rates, i.e., the number of children per woman is slowly but steadily decreasing, which is not the result of birth control programs but only of the courageous, conscious behavior of African women. Unlike other cases of demographic growth in emerging countries, in Africa it would seem that women have been left alone to face the problem, isolating and often blaming them for a society that has not always been prepared for such revolutionary choices. The ruling classes prefer not to talk about birth control and how to implement it, with a few significant exceptions that I am pleased to mention, as this is a topic I consider to be extremely important. A few months ago, the former President of Liberia and Nobel Peace Prize winner Ellen Johnson Sirleaf said in a conference in Italy – as reported by the *Corriere della Sera* on 9 April this year – that Africa must address the problem of birth control in the face of demographic growth forecasts and that it should address it "by promoting education in general and sexual education in particular, and by encouraging girls to stay in school". The former President of the Parliament of Burkina Faso Salif Diallo also spoke out in favor of legislation supporting women and promoting a conscious, controlled birth rate. A few other examples had previously been found in East Africa but also in these cases with no significant follow-up. Indeed, in the last few days, it has emerged that Niger is going to adopt a plan for its population development that could have important consequences. Apart from the valid and appropriate solutions proposed by Sirleaf, I think it is very important that the problem of birth control in Africa be addressed and at such an authoritative level. I believe that too little is being said and, above all, done, except individually, about this problem – the real key to managing development problems and balances in Africa and in the world.

Africa's massive, rapid population growth has had extraordinary consequences, the developments and effects of which are difficult to understand. This has helped overcome one of the main obstacles to the continent's economic, technological and cultural development, namely – as mentioned above – the dispersion of its small population over a vast territory: this made contact, exchange, knowledge acquisition and innovation difficult. There are more and more young people in African society, which therefore tends to magnify the qualities of curiosity, courage, imagination and the search for innovation typical of young people and with an increasingly less incisive presence of the elderly, whose experience and tradition tend to curb this tendency. The effects of this are revolutionary, and we do not know how to measure this completely in cultures that have always been characterized by the cult of the ancestor and by the sometimes-dominant value of traditions and the past. This growing young population, while ensuring the dynamism of the system, requires the continuous adaptation of educational and working structures. It seems difficult, if not impossible, for the majority of African countries to create enough schools and jobs to provide a framework and respond to the needs of this large mass of youth. Africa's imperatives are: resources for extraordinary investments, an adequate number of trainers who have enough preparation, and sufficient time to find both of these while the population is quickly growing. Reflecting on some of these realities and on their dimension would be sufficient, among other things, to express a very robust opinion on international cooperation, which receives less and less funding, while its purpose seems to be stuck in models that are outdated and unsuitable for these changes. This is the same reality from which the migratory flows that so frighten Western public opinion originate. The number of migrants from Africa to Italy and Europe is still low despite the fake news and images dramatically spread by our media showing inflatable boats laden with predominantly African young people trying to cross the Mediterranean. There are currently around a million Africans in Italy (mostly from Mediterranean Africa) out of a population of about 60m. However, demographic growth could increase this phenomenon, thus making its management more complicated unless courageous, adequate, effective and shared policies, most of which are largely well known, are adopted in the countries of origin and in those of arrival.

5. Problems and Prospects of a Growing World

Can these developments justify overcoming that submissive relationship to which Calchi Novati referred and merit the onset of a new international position for Africa and the establishment of a new, different relationship with Europe and the world? However, even without a crystal ball to foresee future scenarios, some considerations seem to emerge and help us to better understand this complex phenomenon.

However, we cannot address this issue without mentioning something that is not as obvious as it seems. Africa is a vast continent of over 30m km^2 (larger than China, India and Europe combined) characterized by great geographical, climatic and anthropological diversity. It has enormous, still largely untapped mineral and natural resources (even though they have been relentlessly pilfered by Europe and the world) and has been arbitrarily divided up into culturally heterogeneous states with administrations imported from afar. These are both strengths and weaknesses, factors of cohesion and division. Yet in recent years, they have become increasingly important as powerful stimuli – for the ruling classes as well as for African intellectuals – to develop "African" responses to the various problems that the management of diversity poses daily. Nor should we forget that in addition to the new problems of demographics, climate change, political modernization, social life and corruption that often accompany the rapid, radical transformation processes in a society, there are also the unsolved problems of the past, which coexists with the present and is often the first and most direct reality of everyday life. Until a few years ago, I would have topped this list with everything related to the painful colonial experience, the cultural plundering and the resulting dependence – both psychological and in terms of collective identity. However, I think this factor is becoming less important for an increasingly younger population, who ignore almost everything about that past, thus suffering less and less from it. This is because there are fewer and fewer surviving witnesses of that world and that past in African society. I believe that the persistence of vast areas of poverty and social exclusion is still today – and will be for many years to come – a central problem for all African societies. This problem is part of a legacy of the past; however, it is difficult to solve without adopting policies that combine the three drivers of change: substantial investment, new and different policies of wealth redistribution and the substantial amount of time needed to change deeply entrenched behaviors. At the moment, I would only like to stress that today – and increasingly so – financial flows to Africa are mainly made up of African workers' remittances from abroad, which generally respond directly to real social and family members' needs without the ambiguities of international aid cooperation flows.

The partly new, partly old issue of armed conflicts, which claims lives and hinders social development in some areas of the continent, certainly deserves separate reflection. These almost always originate from cultural or economic divisions and/or contrasts that are rooted in history and in what remains of ancient identities. In most cases, conflicts are triggered when those diversities turn into a cause for violence and oppression. Traditional African societies had relationships that were sometimes able to help overcome existing, known differences. In some circumstances, today, these mechanisms seem to have been forgotten. To make matters worse, violence is used as an end in itself, as in the contemporary cases of the so-called religious wars, which are becoming more widespread, with the penetration of extremist and violent movements, especially in the Sahel area. Here, however, the source of the conflicts is abroad, the final phase in those manipulations and accentuations of diversity, poverty or ignorance that justify the use of arms. Countries such as Nigeria, Mali, Burkina Faso and Niger are affected by the repeated terrorist activities of armed groups, which take advantage of the situation of utter anarchy and free trade in arms, drugs and human beings now prevailing in post-Gaddafi Libya. However, the threat posed by these armed conflicts and their lack of control should not be underestimated. The fragility of African states and their defense apparatuses sometimes seems to invite violent groups to proceed with weapons in economics as well as in politics. The international community and Europe, first and foremost, has been following these phenomena in a divided and distracted way, in some cases even facilitating them with either its direct intervention or its absence. Libya is certainly the most resounding example, as its devastating consequences attest. However, actions, such as withholding assistance to legitimate institutions and the more or less hidden collusion with armed movements, are destabilizing the continent and are becoming increasingly common, transferring international political and economic competition to Africa. In this respect, Africa needs our attention. We can neither observe these phenomena absent-mindedly nor through narrow contingent interests. We should learn a lesson from the case of the Middle East, devastated by 30 years of terrible wars that have caused hundreds of thousands of deaths; millions of wounded and desperately fleeing refugees; and the destruction of entire cities, infrastructures and economies. These wars do not seem to have paved the way to peace and prospects for reconstruction and re-launching, but only to deep-seated hatred that can cause further violence and the contemporary distortion of the very identity of that region, as is the case of the almost total annihilation of age-old, fundamental cultures and large communities, including the Christian one.

6. A Look at a Possible Future

The reactions of the international community's main players, in the face of these developments in Africa, often, but not always, display the awareness that these are profound, irreversible and large-scale processes that not only deeply modify African society but also international equilibria. China's reaction has been the most wide-ranging and innovative. China entered Africa many years ago with a far-sighted vision which was an indication of future change. From the beginning, the Chinese model focused on creating exchange mechanisms providing its workers with turnkey projects with minimal local involvement in exchange for – as a method of payment – raw materials, of which Africa has an abundance, where China does not. In this form of cooperation, everyone gets something with minimal political, economic and cultural risk. The Chinese preferred cooperation projects, such as large infrastructure, as well as sports facilities and venues for political and cultural events, which were completed especially in exchange for the purchase of oil and its derivatives. However, over the years, the volume of Chinese investment has grown, and Beijing has carved out a very significant position as the key promoter of the continent's development. Behind Africa's rapid growth in GDP mentioned above lies not only a different trend in the international prices of raw materials – especially crude oil – and better economic policies, but also large injections of Chinese capital and, more recently, unprecedented direct and partnership relations between Chinese and African companies. This does not mean that Beijing's presence in Africa is all positive; nor does it allow us to forget the sometimes-destructive effects of cheap Chinese goods in local markets on emergent small African industries. Nor does it allow us to forget the equally dangerous effect of Chinese companies purchasing African land, which is still widely available and inexpensive. This land is also the fundamental reserve of intangible and traditional values of these companies as well as the capital that will support the next great wave of African population growth. Like it or not, Beijing now has a strong presence in Africa, where it advances with the authoritativeness not only of its economic and technological power, but also with the strength of the expertise and experience gained in the field over these years of quiet preparation. For Africa, the Chinese presence opens up prospects for independence and development that so far had only been dreamt of and substantially reduces the role of Europe's presence, which every day risks becoming nothing more than a relic of the past, undermining its historical dominance.

The China-Africa-Europe triangle, with the prospect of the growing influence of India, was the real change on the international scene at the beginning of this century and may have considerable influence on world developments. The United States – focused mainly on satisfying its national interests with President Trump's dominant "America First" strategy and its defense of her main interests in Asia and the Pacific, where competition with China is now more crucial and direct – now seems distanced from the African arena and shows scant interest in the continent's economy and developments.

It is interesting to note that within this triangle, China and Africa represent the factors of growth, bearers of the most significant innovations and transformations, while Europe is currently the weakest element, suffering and unable to take advantage of its economic, political and cultural power. Much is being said and written about this "decadence" of Europe, its causes and its limits, even if this dramatic issue does not sound the social alarm we might expect. In this case too, demographics seem to play a major role. If migrants and their children are excluded, the rump European population is tending to shrink, because generally every year fewer children are born and birth rates are lower than mortality rates. Europe's population lives longer, thanks to ever-better hygiene, nutrition and health conditions, but it is becoming predominantly composed of elderly people, naturally inclined to preserve customs and habits and to fear change and diversity. Therefore, it is a population that tends to fear the future and wants to protect what it has at present. Some of these elements are deeply rooted and are therefore difficult to change, such as the general propensity of European society to have few children, to marry later or not to marry at all. These behaviors result from profound sociocultural changes on which financial incentives have little impact. Others, on the contrary, originate and feed on emotions that are in turn induced by images or propaganda and that can therefore be managed and changed over time. In recent years, we have witnessed the serious political effects – such as Brexit in Great Britain – generated by the exaggerated, unfounded fear of an "invasion" of the island by foreign immigrants who might corrupt their customs and traditions. Here, the past is apparently successfully recalled – even if perhaps only temporary – by political and social forces based on tradition and those values that should be maintained and protected, if anything by raising walls and preventing contamination. Therefore, attitudes of mistrust, closure and return to forms of national preference, like the ones that for centuries afflicted European history and been the cause of the terrible tragedies in the last century, seem to become entrenched. As such, we have two continents on the offensive and one on the defensive, with the Americas and the Middle East focused on their domestic problems and world competition development forecasts. This could be a summary of the European view of the contemporary global arena.

China – with its growing areas of influence in Asia and Africa – shares little in common with the latter, both in terms of historical heritage and cultural roots, but also in terms of current economic magnitude and political and social organizational model. Just think of the simple fact that the Chinese are under a single government, while the Africans are divided into 53 different states, all trying to overcome their differences and coordinate their policies in more or less effective forms of economic and political cooperation. However, both are economic and demographic powers in full and overwhelming expansion. China has already seen its most intense phase of demographic development and is now managing its economic, military and political growth with an iron fist. China's power and expansion strategy moves directly through Asia and Africa toward Europe through two gigantic infrastructure routes, one maritime and one terrestrial, built with colossal financial investments and united under the friendly name of the "New Silk Road" – or more aptly – of the "one belt and one road initiative". New and faster channels will be thus opened to facilitate trade, transforming "distant" China into Europe's next-door "neighbor".

Despite these difficulties for Europe, the game of Euro-African relations still seems to be underway. In Pavia, we launched the theme of African Europe. However, this is not an understanding of Europe invaded by Africans due to the unstoppable flow of mass migrations generated by the enormous, growing demographic and economic gap between the two, nor a Europe that is culturally or economically dominated by Africa. What we were thinking about was a cohesive Europe, finally confident in itself and its strength, but united with Africa in a strong alliance capable of opening up real spaces for political collaboration and economic partnership, in a block whose magnitude could withstand global competition and provide a solution to substantial contemporary problems.

Africa, with its tumultuous development, seems committed to overturning, or at least reducing, the negative power relationship Calchi Novati talked about, one of the main causes of this traditional "lopsided relationship", with the transformation of collaboration into submission. It is now up to Europe to overcome its fears – and lay its ghosts to rest – and rediscover the founding values of its culture, rethink and rebuild its governance structure and give new substance to its dialogue with African societies, starting with those that already have gained residence and citizenship here with us and to whom we will have to offer different forms of integration and participation in our lives. Europe must regain the trust of Africans and build with them viable alternatives to mass migration along with sustainable examples of development and economic collaboration and credible prospects for the better global management of the environmental problems that threaten the world.

The Interplay between the Regional and Sub-regional Dimensions of African Regionalism: A Historical Perspective

Giovanni Finizio

1. Introduction

Africa is the continent with the highest density of regional organizations. A continent-wide organization, the African Union (AU), coexists, interacts, and is supposed to co-operate with many sub-continental organizations which have proliferated over time, giving rise to a highly complex inter-institutional system which has been described as a "Spaghetti-bowl".[1] As Fig. 1 shows, this expression refers to, and provides, a graphical representation of a messy system of overlapping integrative schemes with partially conflicting political and economic paradigms (Tavares and Tang, 2011).[2] This kind of decentralized regionalism is very different from the European concentric integration model, in which a political and economic organization (the European Union), a currency area (the Eurozone), and a border and migration zone (the Schengen Area) partially intersect under the umbrella of the Council of Europe, with 15 member states occupying the center of the picture.[3]

---

[1] The concept of "Spaghetti bowl" was originally proposed by Bhagwati (1995), in order to represent the particular issue of overlapping free trade areas.

[2] While there are currently at least 19 regional and sub-regional organizations in Africa, Fig. 1 includes only the eight Regional Economic Communities (RECs) formally recognized and supported by the AU as building blocks of regional integration (cfr. Section 5.1 below).

[3] *Mutatis mutandis*, similar considerations can be applied to other systems of regional integration. For the Latin American case, see Malamud and Gardini (2012).

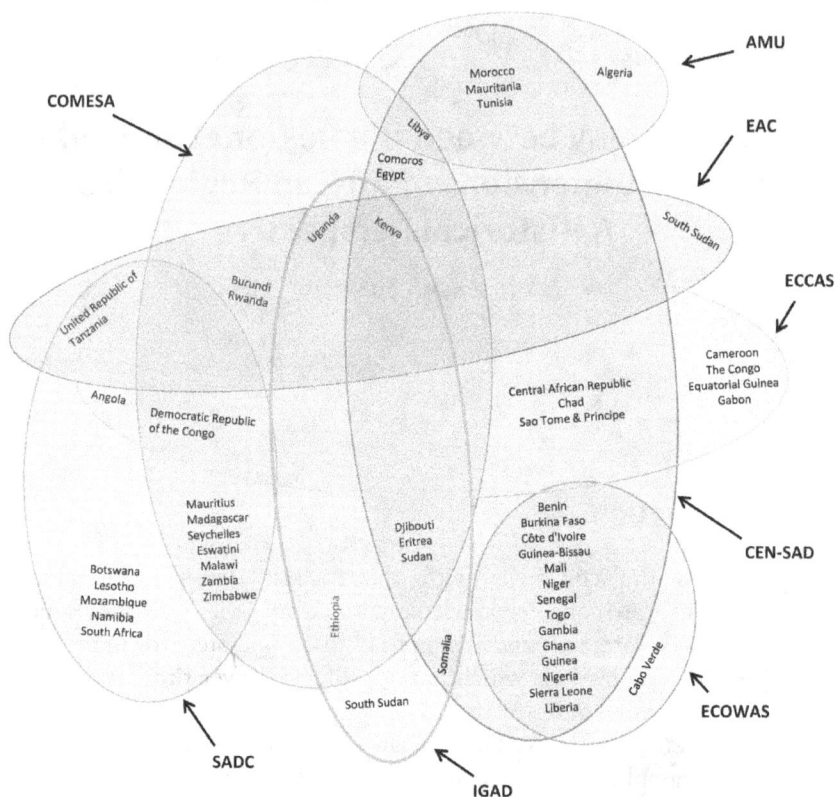

Fig. 1. Decentralized regionalism and overlapping membership in African regional economic communities (RECs).
Source: UNCTAD (2019, p. 8).

Such a disorganized system resembles to some extent the disorder of global governance and heavily undermines the effectiveness of African regionalism.

The Organization of African Unity (OAU, replaced in 2002 by the AU) was originally mainly entrusted with political tasks and only later became increasingly active in the economic field.[4] In contrast, most

---

[4] Although in 1963 the OAU was endowed with an Economic and Social Commission to foster economic cooperation in Africa, especially in the early years, the Organization was mainly focused on political objectives such as decolonization, the protection

sub-regional organizations, established to cooperate in the economic realm, in the 1990s started to become relevant as political and security actors. As these institutions gradually began to operate in the same fields of activity, coordination and co-operation between them gained more and more importance, and became a crucial dimension of the rationalization of the whole regional integration system which many call for.

This chapter discusses the relations between the "continental" (or "regional") and sub-continental (or sub-regional) levels of African regionalism, presenting their features, limits, and future challenges. It is organized as follows: the first two sections present the historical roots of this two-level institutional system of regional governance; the third provides the reader with the endogenous and exogenous factors which engendered and fuel it; the last section is focused on the evolution of relations between the OAU/AU and sub-regional organizations in the economic and security fields.

2. Historical Roots of the Continental/Sub-regional System of African Regionalism

The dynamics between the continental and sub-regional dimensions of African regionalism have their roots in the birth of the ideal of African unity and its transformation into a political movement in the context of European colonialism. After World War II, Pan-Africanism,[5] led by a young generation of activists and ideologists such as George Padmore, Jomo Kenyatta, and Kwame Nkrumah, started to pursue the economic, political and military unification of the territories undergoing decolonization *on a continental and supranational basis.* The establishment of a kind of United States of Africa was considered as the only way to ensure the effective emancipation of newly independent African states from the neo-colonial pressures of European and industrial powers, and

---

of member states' sovereignty and the cooperation among them for a common projection on the international arena (Legum, 1964).

[5]   Pan-Africanism can be defined as a political ideology based on the realization of the fragmented nature of the existence of Africans, their marginalization and alienation both on the continent and in the Diaspora, and affirms the consequent need to promote their unity and solidarity for a future of emancipation, development and peace (Murithi, 2005, p. 7).

to promote security and development for the continent (Nkrumah, 1963, p. 174).

However, this objective of Pan-Africanists, continental in scope, had to come to terms with the dynamics of unification that had already affected some African regions under colonial rule. France and Great Britain, in particular, had promoted some integration among their administrative units, on the one hand increasing intra-bloc interdependence (through a common language, common markets, common infrastructures) and on the other hand establishing common institutions to manage it. In East Africa, for instance, British colonial power proved to be "the deepest unifying factor" (Franck 1964, p. 9). As early as the late 19th century, white settlers urged federation, their aim being a white dominion reaching to the Rhodesias and dominated by Kenya (Cox 1964, p. 36). After WWII Great Britain launched a High Commission, later replaced by the East African Common Services Organization (EACSO), to manage common services (collection of taxes, posts and telecommunications, railways, airline company, and meteorological services), the common market which was developed between 1922 and 1949 and the common currency among countries undergoing decolonization (Massell 1963, p. 29). In Central and West Africa, France had organized its colonies into two large federations – French Equatorial Africa and French West Africa, established in 1902 and 1904 respectively – with the aim to coordinate, within larger frameworks, the activities of these territories, bestowing on them a degree of autonomy while keeping them under control (Julienne 1967, p. 339).

While Africa was organized in different microcosms linked to, and dependent on, their respective metropoles, interdependence and connections between them were kept rather loose. Not surprisingly, Pan-Africanists, while holding continental unity as a long-term goal, were induced by realistic considerations to elaborate plans for the establishment of sub-regional federations as first steps toward African unity (Padmore 1956, p. 22). Moreover, after the independence of African countries, their natural reflex was to establish sub-regional organizations, rather than a continent-wide integration scheme. In East Africa, Pan-Africanist Julius Nyerere, together with Jomo Kenyatta and Tom Mboya,[6] led a large mixed grouping of political parties and states of

---

[6] After independence, Nyerere would become the President of Tanganika (later Tanzania), while Kenyatta and Mboya would become the President and Minister of

the region pursuing the creation of an East African Federation,[7] paving the way to the launch of the East African Community (EAC) in 1967. In British West Africa, some transnational movements (the West African National Congress) had, since the 1920s, pursued the unification of the four British territories (Ghana, Nigeria, Sierra Leone, and Gambia) on a federal basis, while others (the Pan-African Federation and the West African National Secretariat) called for the unity of the whole region including Francophone countries (Welch, 1966, p. 17).

In the Francophone colonial and post-colonial world, the approach toward integration was quite different. The French branch of Pan-Africanism, based in Paris and active since the 1930s, as well as the African leaders in the territories ruled by France, did not share the militant and radical approach to African unity expressed by Nkrumah and his fellow Anglophones. This was due to the particular relations between France and its colonies. Unlike Great Britain, Paris adopted a centralized system of colonial rule based on assimilation. This approach aimed to integrate the colonies into the French constitutional system as overseas dependencies and their inhabitants into the French legal and cultural system (Manning 1998, pp. 70, 79). As a consequence, France imposed the absolute standardization of political, economic, social and cultural models in all colonies, without taking into consideration the differences among their populations (Wallerstein, 1961, p. 66). Many African leaders in the French possessions, such as Leopold Senghor and Felix Houphoët-Boigny, acquired high political positions in Paris and cemented their relations with the central power through individual concessions for personal advancement. As a consequence, they were not too eager to stand up to the colonial authorities. Moreover, even once independence was gained, they were more inclined to defend the preservation of a strong interdependence with (or dependence on) Paris.

Not surprisingly, soon after independence, Francophone countries in West and Central Africa formed exclusive sub-regional organizations supported by France. Even today, organizations such as UEMOA and CEMAC[8] problematically coexist and overlap in their sub-regions with more comprehensive organizations such as ECOWAS and ECCAS,

---

Justice of Kenya, respectively.

[7] Pan-African Movement for East, Central and Southern Africa (PAFMECSA).

[8] UEMOA and CEMAC are the French acronyms of West Africa Economic and Monetary Union, and Central African Economic and Monetary Community,

which transcend the political and linguistic cleavages inherited from the colonial period.

3. Regionalism vs. Sub-regionalism: The Political Debate after the Independence of African States

In the early 1960s, the common front of African independent States became fragmented over the issue of African unity, spawning two main political blocs. The "Casablanca Group", established in 1961 and led by Nkrumah, was composed of radical states actively supporting, or at least open to, the immediate political unification of the continent along supranational lines, in order to put an end to the *divide et impera* and neo-colonialist policies of western powers.[9] Furthermore, Nkrumah in particular was strongly against any fragmentation of the continent into politico-ideological blocs linked to the former colonial powers, and any gradualism in African unification based on functional sub-regional organizations. According to this position, bloc or functional organizations would have allowed the neo-colonial forces to organize and perpetuate relationships of dependence with former colonies and make any real African unity and independence virtually impossible. In stark contrast, the "Monrovia Group",[10] created in 1962 and composed of more conservative leaders including the Francophones, was basically against severing their relationships with former colonial powers and considered African unity as a mere search for cohesion and solidarity among independent and sovereign African countries, rather than a supranational political construction.[11] For these countries, continental political unity was neither desirable nor possible in the short term, and African unity would have to take the form of a continental

---

respectively. On the history of CEMAC and ECCAS cfr. Meyer (2014a and 2014b). On the problematic coexistence of ECOWAS and UEMOA cfr. Asante (2004).

[9]   The Group was composed of Morocco, United Arab Republic, Ghana, Guinea, Mali and Provisional Government of the Algerian Republic.

[10] The Group comprised 20 countries: Libya, Tunisia, Liberia, Nigeria, Sierra Leone, Togo, Somalia, Ethiopia, Benin, Upper Volta, Cameroon, Central African Republic, Chad, Congo (Brazzaville), Ivory Coast, Gabon, Madagascar, Mauritania, Niger and Senegal.

[11] The description of the two groups provided here is necessarily schematic and oversimplified. For a detailed discussion on this cfr. Thompson (1969, pp. 162 ff.).

intergovernmental organization accompanied by gradual and functional cooperation/integration processes at the sub-regional level.

At the Conference of Addis Ababa in 1963, which established the OAU, the Monrovia Group's approach prevailed. The new organization was strictly intergovernmental and based on the respect and protection of national sovereignty, on sovereign equality of member states, and on the principle of non-interference in their domestic affairs. Moreover, it paved the way to the building of functional sub-regional organizations, leaving political unity as a possible, long-term objective.

However, in Addis Ababa, most countries shared the view that the OAU was incompatible with closed blocs of a political-ideological nature and called for the suppression of any pre-existing sub-regional groupings or organizations which had divided African states, such as the Monrovia and Casablanca blocs, PAFMECSA, and the Union Africaine et Malgache (UAM).[12] As a consequence, the Council of Ministers of Dakar, in August 1963, established that "any regional grouping or sub-regional groupings be in keeping with the Charter of the OAU and meet the following criteria: a) [to be based on] geographical realities and economic, social and cultural factors; b) [to co-ordinate] economic, social and cultural activities peculiar to the States concerned".[13]

While the leader of Ghana, Kwame Nkrumah, continued to oppose the sub-regional route to African unity, warning that "regional associations and territorial groupings can only be other forms of balkanization unless they are conceived within the framework of a continental [political and supranational] union" (cit. in Sanger, 1964, p. 274), it became generally accepted among African countries that, given the extreme extension and diversity of the African continent, as well as the heritage of past political factors, the development of sub-regional organizations was the only possible approach to African

---

[12]   UAM was born in September 1961 as an institutionalization of the "Brazzaville Group", comprising all conservative Francophone countries. This organization reproduced the ties among African Francophone territories of the colonial period, but on a much looser integrative basis (Tevoedjre, 1965, pp. 10–11). The members of the group were: Benin, Upper Volta (Burkina Faso), Cameroon, Central African Republic, Chad, Congo (Brazzaville), Ivory Coast, Gabon, Madagascar, Mauritania, Niger and Senegal. Mali and Guinea refused to join the group and established together with Nkrumah the Ghana-Guinea-Mali Union (or Union of African States; August 1961).

[13]   OAU Doc. CM/Res. 5(1), 10 August 1963.

unity. Even the UN Economic Commission for Africa (ECA), which initially had supported the construction of economic regionalism at the continental level, aligned with the new trend, decentralized its structure and put its technical expertise at states' disposal to establish effective sub-regional economic organizations (Gruhn 1979).

As neither the OAU nor the ECA were endowed with the powers to steer the construction of a rational institutional system, however, this gave rise to an uncontrolled proliferation of sub-regional organizations, leading to the current *Spaghetti Bowl.*

4. The Current Picture of African Regionalism: Endogenous and Exogenous Factors

The complexity of African regionalism, defined by the former Chairperson of the AU, Alpha Oumar Konaré, as a "cacophony" (Murithi and Ndinga-Muvumba 2008, p. 11), has been fueled by many factors, some endogenous and others exogenous to the African context.

Among the endogenous factors are the very characteristics of the African States and of the African inter-state system. It is widely known that the model of the centralized and bureaucratic state was imported to Africa by colonizers and then applied to the new African states. While in Europe the construction of modern states took centuries, in Africa the high expectations from newly acquired independence, and from the nationalist leaders, required a rapid construction of strong and effective states, able to provide "fast-track" development, welfare, and security (Warner, 2001, p. 86). However, this endeavor proved to be quite difficult because of the very characteristics of the post-colonial states. Firstly, their borders had been drawn by colonial powers according to their own interests, disregarding any ethnic, linguistic, cultural, and religious considerations and any pre-colonial affinities or loyalties. This arbitrary partitioning prevented many states from having adequate consolidation in terms of effectiveness, an ability to command loyalty from their citizens and govern such diverse societies. Furthermore, this process laid the foundations for structural instability. Secondly, in many cases, these conditions gave rise to small and unviable states, exposed to dangerous security threats. In other words, the decolonization process had launched on the international scene many poor, weak, and artificial states.

In this difficult context, popular expectations from the new regimes became very quickly frustrated, and the exercise of effective jurisdiction over national territories became more and more difficult.[14] Territorial integrity and the very survival of the states became the most pressing concerns of political leaders throughout Africa. These factors fueled a concentration of power in the hands of Presidents and a general regression of many new states into dictatorship. An additional consequence was the personification of political authority which ended up being based on patrimonial networks and patronage (neo-patrimonialism).

Such considerations provide some basic explanations for characteristics of African regionalism, which has been defined by some authors as a "regime-boosting regionalism" (Söderbaum 2007, pp. 192–195). According to them, African leaders are inclined to promote the creation of regional institutions with the main aim of obtaining legitimacy for themselves and their remaining in power, without expressing much concern about their effectiveness. The *laudatio* of regionalism, the conclusion of multiple agreements, and the proliferation of regional summits, often funded by external donors, are described as symbolic practices aimed to strengthen the images of leaders and of the profile of their regimes. Therefore, although the overlapping of organizations and sub-regional agreements obstructs effective and orderly integration, many African leaders do not perceive this as an issue. Rather, multiple membership in many regional organizations is considered as an "opportunit[y] for the pursuit of conference diplomacy [and] participation in externally funded ventures" (Bach, 2005, p. 183).

Interferences by external actors are also very important to explain the "institutional cacophony" mentioned by Konaré. France has played an integrative role for Francophone countries, but has systematically prevented any attempt at building effective sub-regional organizations transcending colonial cleavages, and therefore has hindered any rationalization of the whole system. In West Africa, for instance, Nigeria, with the technical support of the ECA, promoted ECOWAS in 1975 as an exercise of regional leadership with the aim of promoting economic development through regional planning and emancipation from external

---

[14] Not by chance, African states have been defined by Jackson (1990) as *quasi-states*, i.e., states which enjoy external sovereignty and are recognized as sovereign by the international community, but are not able to exert effectively their jurisdiction over their territories and provide their citizens with basic public goods.

forces (France in particular). It comprised (and still does today) all 15 West African countries and was the first attempt to overcome linguistic and colonial separation between Anglophone and Francophone countries. Paris, on the other hand, promoted and actively supported first the Communauté Economique de l'Afrique de l'Ouest (CEAO) and then UEMOA, both involving only Francophone countries, in order to keep them under its influence and oppose Nigerian leadership ambitions.

Even today, the two overlapping and competing organizations partially share the same objectives and competences, but UEMOA presents more supranational characteristics and is more effective than ECOWAS.[15] The former enjoys the direct political, economic, and technical support of France and the EU (Commission Européenne 1997), and its integrative project is based on the monetary union made possible by the participation of its member countries in the CFA monetary zone, managed by Paris and linked to the Euro. Not by chance, its structure and powers resemble to some extent the EU's normative instruments and institutional model (Claeys, Sindzingre 2003).

EU trade strategies also can complicate the rationalization of African regionalism. Since the 1960s, the EU has been widely recognized as the most important supporter of African regionalism (Telò 2014), but over the last two decades has contributed to some extent to making it more disorganized. The Cotonou Agreement, signed in 2000 by the EU and the ACP countries, launched the project of concluding seven Economic Partnership Agreements (EPAs; five in Africa, one in the Pacific and one in the Caribbean region) by 2008, establishing as many South-South-North free trade areas coherent with WTO rules and based on the reciprocity principle (Meyn 2012, pp. 198–199.). This venture is part of the EU's attempt to promote partner countries' development by gradually integrating them into the world economy. After the signing and the entry into force of the first EPA with the Caribbean countries, however, the negotiation and ratification processes encountered resistance by many African states. Among the many criticisms of the EPAs was the fact that groupings of states envisaged by the EPAs in many cases did not coincide with the existing sub-regional organizations, making the *Spaghetti Bowl*

---

[15] According to a report released by ECOWAS Secretariat, for instance, in 1998 only 45 % of ECOWAS programs have been implemented by its member states, compared to 68 % of UEMOA programs by its members (ECOWAS 1998; see also Gandois 2014, pp. 203–205).

even more complex.[16] Although the EU recognized the problem,[17] and as early as 2007 committed itself to support, together with the AU, the integration of different sub-regional organizations making it compatible with the EPAs process (Council of the European Union, 2007, para. 99), the current situation is still difficult.

5. The Relations between the OAU/AU and Sub-regional Organizations

Sub-regional organizations have proliferated after the birth of the OAU and independently from it. Initially, they were established for economic purposes but then, particularly in the 1990s, most of them were relaunched on multi-dimensional bases and entrusted with wider competences in fields such as peace, security, and democracy promotion. In contrast, the OAU was mainly endowed with political objectives (such as the preservation of the sovereignty of African States, cooperation among them for a common projection on the international arena, and support for the decolonization process)[18] and became increasingly active in the field of economic cooperation. This factor, together with the increasing need of rationalization of the whole institutional picture, implied a pursuit of effective cooperation between the continental and sub-regional organizations.

5.1. The interplay between the OAU/AU and sub-regional organizations in the economic field

The issue of cooperation between the OAU and sub-regional organizations in the economic field was addressed by the former, in conjunction with the ECA, as early as 1980, when the Assembly convened an extraordinary session to discuss the economic problems of the continent. The adoption of the *Lagos Plan of Action for the Economic Development of Africa 1980–2000* (LPA; Fashole and Shaw 1984), complemented by

---

[16] In Southern Africa, for instance, members of Southern African Development Community (SADC) belong to three different EPA groupings.

[17] Cfr., for instance, the document by Luis Michel (2008), at the time Commissioner for Development and Humanitarian Aid.

[18] Cfr. note 4.

the Final Act of Lagos (FLA), set up a new paradigm for the economic development of the continent. In particular, it put forward the argument that the vulnerability of African economies to their external environment was the immediate cause of their underdevelopment. Instead of pursuing a strategy based on the centrality of trade of primary goods, it was necessary to integrate national economies and build continental and sub-regional markets for an African economic order. This order was to be based on *collective self-reliance, self-sustainment*, democratization of the development process and a fair distribution of the fruits of development (Adedeji, 2004, p. 261). The LPA and FLA expressed States' commitment to establish by 2000 an *African Economic Community* (AEC) to ensure economic, cultural, and social integration for the continent. To this aim, for the 1980s, the Heads of State and Government decided for a path including the strengthening of existing sub-regional organizations, the creation of new ones where needed, and their coordination; and for the 1990s, the implementation of an African common market. To this end, the ECA divided Africa into five sub-regions in which to build as many *Regional Economic Communities* (RECs) transcending linguistic colonial cleavages.

The AEC integration process was launched by the 1991 Abuja Treaty, which entered into force in 1994 and envisaged, within 34 years, the free movement of people and of production factors, the creation of a single market, an economic and monetary union, a central bank, and a single currency at the end of a six-step continental integration process in which the RECs would be building blocks (Bach, 2005, p. 175).[19] To this end, the 1998 Protocol on Relations between the AEC and the RECs promoted horizontal coordination among RECs and provided an institutional structure enabling the EAC Secretariat to harmonize programs and policies for the realization of EAC objectives. It also established that the RECs reviewed their statutes to recognize the realization of AEC as a final goal and to be absorbed into the African common market at the end of the process[20].

The AU, replacing the OAU in 2000, took on the management of the EAC continental integration process and the task of coordinating the

---

[19] *Treaty Establishing the African Economic Community*, art. 6.

[20] *Protocol on Relations between the African Economic Community and the Regional Economic Communities*, 1998, art. 3 and 5.

RECs. The AU Constitutive Act provided the objective of harmonization and coordination of policies between "the existing and future Regional Economic Communities" (art. 3(I)). According to the AU Constitutive Act, the RECs were expected to be subordinated to the continental organization and to rationalize their agendas and operations "for the gradual attainment of the objectives of the Union". This was effectively requested to the RECs by the new Protocol of 2007 on Relations between the AU and RECs. In the meantime, in 2006, in order to discourage the further proliferation of sub-regional organizations, the AU Summit held in Gambia decided to recognize and support only eight RECs as building blocks of regional integration (ECOWAS, Common Market for Eastern and Southern Africa (COMESA), EAC, ECCAS, Southern African Development Community (SADC), Intergovernmental Authority for Development (IGAD), Arab Maghreb Union (AMU), Economic Community of Sahelo-Saharian States (CEN-SAD)) and established a moratorium on the creation of new sub-regional organizations.[21]

RECs were supposed to generate more intra-regional trade between the member states, based on competitiveness and the creation of larger markets. Unfortunately, this has occurred rather slowly and unevenly, because of their difficulty in removing "tariff and non-tariff barriers, as a result of multiple membership in different RECs with conflicting or overlapping standards, procedures and obligations, and [difficulty in] coordinat[ing] and harmoniz[ing] extra-community import policies in key sectors" (African Union, 2007, para. 352; Apuuli, 2016, pp. 150–151). In addition, many RECs are still affected by enforcement problems. The absence of strong supranational institutions to ensure strict compliance and the lack of enforcement mechanisms to sanction noncompliant states make it difficult to implement trade liberalization and other integration measures (Akonor, 2010, p. 82). The Abuja Treaty of 1991 assumed that RECs would all conduct economic integration programs to become customs unions within 23 years of the entry to force of the treaty, i.e., by 2017. That did not happen, and different RECs have divergent integration timelines (ECA, AU, ADB, UNCTAD, 2019, p. 48).

African leaders have recognized these problems and in 2012 fast-tracked the establishment of the Continental Free Trade Area

---

[21] AU Assembly, *Decision on the Moratorium on the Recognition of Regional Economic Communities*, 1–2 July 2006, AU Doc, Assembly/AU/Dec.112 (VII).

(CFTA).[22] The Treaty establishing it, brokered by the AU, was signed on 21 March 2018, "lay[ing] the foundation for the establishment of a Continental Customs Union at a later stage" and the "creat[ion] of a single market". CFTA came into force on 30 May 2019 and, as of today, it has been signed by 54 out of 55 AU member countries. The Treaty has now to face the difficult challenge of implementation and operationalization which, again, is closely connected to the issue of multiple REC membership, the effective harmonization of RECs and their rationalization.

Currently, there are four functioning free trade areas by AU-recognized RECs: COMESA, ECOWAS, EAC, and SADC. In addition, further intra-African trade is liberalized through mechanisms beyond the AU-recognized RECs, including the Pan-Arab free trade area, CEMAC, and the Southern African Customs Union (SACU; ECA, AU, ADB 2017, p. 35). Some steps toward integration among RECs have been taken. In June 2015, COMESA, the EAC, and SADC created the Tripartite Free Trade Area (TFTA), based on the assumption that the three organizations would "start working towards a merger into a single REC".[23] This did not happen, however. Since the tripartite integration process is based on the principle of "building on the REC acquis", the TFTA evolved to represent, in at least the short to medium term, a new layer of FTAs over the three RECs, rather than a consolidation (ECA, AU, ADB 2017, p. 56).

As of today, only 12 African countries belong to a single REC; 33 belong to 2 RECs, 8 to 3 RECs, and 1 to 4 RECs (ECA, AU, ADB, UNCTAD 2019, p. 49), which complicates the advancement of deeper continental economic integration. For these reasons, an explicit objective of the CFTA is to "resolve the challenges of multiple and overlapping memberships and expedite the regional and continental integration processes".[24] However, as Article 19 of the CFTA agreement allows the REC trading arrangements to persist as islets of deeper integration within the CFTA system, the Continental Free Trade Area does not, in the short term, consolidate the REC FTAs. In addition, the AU does not have any

---

[22] *Decision on Boosting Intra-African Trade and Fast-Tracking the Continental Free Trade Area*, EX.CL/700(XX), Assembly/AU/Dec.394(XVIII), 29–30 January 2012.

[23] *Final Communique of the COMESA-EAC-SADC Tripartite Summit*, October 2008.

[24] *Decision on Boosting Intra-African Trade and Fast-Tracking the Continental Free Trade Area*, cit.

central power to impose effectiveness, convergence, and rationalization on RECs.

The CFTA thus fosters liberalization across the continent but does not conclusively address the issues posed by membership in overlapping trading regimes; it does not fully consolidate Africa's fragmented markets into a single regime, but instead leaves a web of better connected but distinct trade regimes. Nevertheless, by liberalizing trade between these regimes, the CFTA functions as an intermediate step toward their later consolidation (ECA, AU, ADB, UNCTAD 2019, p. 54).

5.2. *The interplay between the OAU/AU and sub-regional organizations in the security field*

After the end of the Cold War, all RECs recognized by the AU gradually developed the institutional capacity to also address security-related issues. On the one hand, this was the consequence of the proliferation of violent conflicts in the different sub-regions of the continent; on the other hand, an important role was played by the diffusion of an ideological paradigm based on political and economic liberalism. The new climate, favored by the increasing interdependence brought by globalization, was reflected in UN discourse, which clearly stated the interdependence and indivisibility of development, democracy, human rights, peace, and security.[25]

Moreover, at least two of the major crises of the 1990s had occurred in Africa (Somalia and Rwanda), and it was clear that, after the Cold War, the international community was reluctant to employ human, political, and economic resources to tackle increasingly complex crises on a continent which had lost its strategic relevance. The United Nations and the multilateral system, on the other hand, had proved to be inadequate in a dramatically changed world. Therefore, it became increasingly evident that the Africans would have to bear the primary responsibility to ensure peace in the continent ("try Africa first").

However, in the 1990s, the limits of the OAU in the maintenance of peace and security had been laid bare by the proliferation of the "new

---

[25] Cfr. the three documents which marked the mandate of the Secretary-general Boutros Boutros-Ghali: *An Agenda for Peace* (1992), *An Agenda for Development* (1994), *An Agenda for Democratization* (1996).

wars",[26] which had become the rule in Africa. In fact, an organization based on non-interference was structurally ill equipped to tackle them, and member states felt the need to set up a new *ad hoc* institutional architecture.[27]

With the AU, the new African Peace and Security Architecture (APSA) was established. At the heart of the APSA is a 15-member Peace and Security Council (PSC), entrusted with making decisions on conflict prevention and peace-building and supported by, among other bodies, the African Stand-by Force and the Continental Early Warning System, all implying a close synergy between the AU and RECs.

The Protocol establishing the PSC recognized the contribution of Regional Mechanisms (RM) in the maintenance of peace, security, and stability; stated that they were part of the overall security architecture of the Union; and called for a harmonization and coordination of activities with these Mechanisms to ensure effective partnership, taking account of "comparative advantage of each and the prevailing circumstances" (art. 7 and 16). In effect, "by the proximity to the theatres of regional conflicts, the RECs tend to display a good understanding of the causes and dynamics of these conflicts. They also often have strong incentives to respond promptly to conflicts in their respective neighbourhoods" (Nagar and Ngaje, 2018, p. 217).

In January 2008, the AU and RECs signed a Memorandum of Understanding with the objective of institutionalizing and strengthening their cooperation and the coordination of their activities in the peace and security field. They also committed to "contribute to the full operationalization and effective functioning" of APSA, based on the principles of subsidiarity, comparative advantage, and complementarity (Touray, 2016, p. 77). The concrete application of these principles has proved to be problematic, however. While, according to the PSC

---

[26] Mary Kaldor (1999) called "new wars" civil wars with elements of transnationality, whose main victims (and targets), in contrast to traditional inter-state wars, are the civilians and not the military.

[27] This necessity had been already recognized in 1990 by the *Declaration on the Political and Socio-Economic Situation in Africa and the Fundamental Changes Taking Place in the World* (OAU Doc. AHG/Decl. 1 (XXVI), but OAU, albeit updated and strengthened by the creation of the Mechanism for Conflict Prevention, Management and Resolution (MCPMR), had shown all of its inadequacy. Just consider the fact that the only peacekeeping operation deployed by the OAU, in 1981–82 in Chad, led to a failure (Sesay, 1999).

Protocol, the AU is supposed to exert primacy in maintaining peace and security in Africa, RECs "like ECOWAS and SADC that established security mechanisms before the AU was born – and, as in the case of ECOWAS, have solid peacekeeping experience – often feel that the AU has more to learn from them rather than vice-versa" (Adebajo, 2008, p. 134). In general terms, both the AU and the RECs are based on autonomous treaties and no relation of subordination can be envisaged. As a consequence, although some RECs have made attempts to coordinate their activities and the communications between the AU and RECs have been improved through the appointment of REC/RM Liaison Officers to the partner organizations, the relationships have been often inspired by competition, rather than cooperation. This is due to the fact that all organizations are primarily vehicles through which member states pursue their interests and "the extent to which cooperation and coordination takes place within and between these organizations depend to a large extent on national interest calculations and the prevailing balance of power among member states" (Nagar and Ngaje, 2018, p. 225). In any given conflict situation, states will prioritize the authority of either the AU or an REC, not out of a careful assessment of the conflict dynamics and the capabilities of that organization to respond appropriately, but mostly on the basis of which organization affords them enough space to legitimize their preferred approach to resolving the conflict (ibid.).

Furthermore, in order to make any inter-institutional cooperation effective and useful, actors involved have to be reliable. Sub-regional organizations are generally affected by weak capacities. Most of them are poorly run, with poor leadership which lacks an overall vision or plan of action (Söderbaum, Hettne 2010, pp. 24–28). The personnel lack the right training, education, and experience to perform the duties they are assigned (Makinda, Okumu and Mickler 2016, p. 129). Of course, the overlapping of sub-regional institutions and mechanisms in the field of peace and security also does not help, as member countries are hardly able to invest adequate resources in all organizations they are involved in. Nor does it help the interference of external actors (like France), which can try to orient the approach of a sub-regional organization toward a particular crisis, in order to pursue their interests.[28]

---

[28] A case in point is, for instance, the attempt by France to shape ECOWAS' response to the political crisis of 2001 in Ivory Coast (Nagar and Ngaje, 2016, p. 226).

An additional problem is that the national interests of powerful member states with hegemonic ambitions sometimes interfere with sub-regional peace efforts, causing internal divisions, organizational paralysis, and biased interventions. For instance, the interventions of ECOWAS promoted by Nigeria in Sierra Leone in 1997, as well as the intervention of South Africa in Lesotho in 1998 under the aegis of SADC have been harshly criticized by other members of both organizations for being driven by hegemonic aspirations and national interests (Francis, 2017, p. 163; Matlosa, 2007, p. 113).

6. Conclusions

As suggested by the ECA, Africa's governance, peace, and security challenges are inextricably linked and are prerequisites to establishing a continent-wide economic space (ECA, AU, ADB, UNCTAD 2019, p. 31). Both African economic architecture and the APSA are supposed to be driven by the AU and to be based on sub-regional organizations as their building blocks. Early proposals made by some radical Pan-Africanists had called for a supranational and truly continent-wide political, economic, and military Union. However, historical factors have led to the construction of an intergovernmental organization at the continental level – the OAU, replaced by the AU in 2002 – and a proliferation of overlapping sub-regional institutions, which induced the former AU Chairperson Konaré to define African regionalism as a "cacophony". Both political elites and the literature have widely recognized that this disorganized system needs to be harmonized and rationalized in order to be effective and respond to Africans' development and security needs. In both the economic and the peace and security realms, a double process of organization has taken place, at the continental and at sub-regional level. And in both realms, the AU is supposed to lead an integration process based on the RECs as building blocks, which should be fully harmonized and associated to the integrative effort. In the economic field, the treaty launching the CFTA has entered into force as an intermediate step toward a common market and a monetary union. In the security field, the APSA was launched in 2002 as an instrument to deal with conflict dynamics, to tackle security challenges, and to promote peace and sustainable development on the continent (Degila, Amegan 2019, p. 393).

In both cases, RECs are considered to work as building blocks of an integration process which could lead, in the long run, to an economic and political union.

Both the AU and the RECs remain, however, independent intergovernmental institutions composed of sovereign states which use them to pursue their national interests. As a consequence, the AU has not been endowed with the power to impose any rationalization of the complex system of overlapping sub-regional organizations; RECs are still weak institutions affected by enforcement problems and cooperation with the AU remains problematic. While CFTA is expected to "resolve the challenges of multiple and overlapping memberships and expedite the regional and continental integration processes", it does not seem, in the short term, to consolidate the REC FTAs and to conclusively address the issues posed by membership in overlapping trading regimes. The CFTA does not fully consolidate Africa's fragmented markets into a single regime, but instead leaves a web of better connected but distinct sub-regional trade regimes. In the field of security, relations between the AU and RECs seem to be inspired more by competition than by cooperation and complementarity.

Both CFTA and APSA are important steps in a process which, however, should not be assessed against the European regional integration experience. In fact, the analysis provided in this chapter suggests that the characteristics of African regionalism and of the interplay between its regional and sub-regional dimensions are rooted in the particular history of the continent. Moreover, they have been deeply affected by external actors and pressures, which in many cases proved to be divisive or not functional to the orderly development of effective African regionalism. This process needs and deserves international support. A more coherent policy by the EU and its member states (France included) which supports APSA, CFTA, the strengthening of EU/RECs cooperation, and the rationalization of African regionalism would greatly help.

References

Adebajo A. (2008), *The Peacekeeping Travails of the AU and the Regional Economic Communities*, in J. Akokpari, and A. Ndinga-Muvumba (eds.), *The African Union and Its Institutions*, Auckland Park: Fanele, pp. 131–161.

Adedeji A. (2004), *The ECA: Forging a Future for Africa*, in Y. Barthelot (ed.), *Unity and Diversity in Development Ideas. Perspectives from the UN Regional Commissions*, Bloomington: Indiana University Press, pp. 233–306.

African Union (2007), *Audit of the African Union: Towards a People-Centered Political and Socio-economic Transformation of Africa*, Addis Ababa.

Akonor K. (2010), *African Economic Institutions*, London and New York: Routledge.

Apuuli K. P. (2016), *The African Union and Regional Integration in Africa*, in D. H. Levine and D. Nagar (eds.), *Region-Building in Africa. Political and Economic Challenges*, Houndmills: Palgrave, pp. 143–156.

Asante S. K. B. (2004), *The Travails of Integration*, in A. Adebajo and I. Rashid (eds.), *West Africa's Security Challenges: Building Peace in a Troubled Region*, Boulder: Lynne Rienner, pp. 51–68.

Bach D. (2005), *The Global Politics of Regionalism: Africa*, in M. Farrell, B. Hettne, and L. van Langenhove (eds.), *Global Politics of Regionalism: Theory and Practice*, London: Pluto Press, pp. 171–185.

Bhagwati J. (1995), *US Trade Policy: The Infatuation of Free Trade Agreements*, in J. Bhagwati, and A. O. Krueger (eds.), *The Dangerous Drift to Preferential Trade Agreements*, Washington: AEI Press, pp. 1–18.

Claeys A.-S., Sidzingre A. (2003), *Regional Integration as a Transfer of Rules: The Case of the Relationship between the European Union and the West African Economic and Monetary Union (WAEMU)*, Development Studies Association Annual Conference, Glasgow, 10–12 September.

Commission Européenne (1997), *L'Union européenne, les États d'Afrique de l'Ouest et l'UEMOA*, Luxembourg, Decembre.

Cox R. (1964), *Pan-Africanism in Practice: PAFMECSA 1958–1964*, London: Oxford University Press.

Council of the European Union (1997), *The Africa-EU Strategic Partnership: A Joint Africa-EU Strategy*, Lisbon, 9 December.

Degila D. E., Amegan C. K. (2019), *The African Peace and Security Architecture: An African Response to Regional Peace and Security Challenges*, in A. Kulnazarova, and V. Popovski (eds.), *The Palgrave Handbook of Global Approaches to Peace*, Houndmills: Palgrave, pp. 393–409.

ECA, AU, ADB (2017), *Assessing Regional Integration in Africa*, Vol. VIII: *Bringing the Continental Free Trade Area About*, Addis Ababa: ECA.

ECA, AU, ADB, UNCTAD (2019), *Assessing Regional Integration in Africa*, Vol. XIX: *Next Steps for the African Continental Free Trade Area*, Addis Ababa: ECA.

ECOWAS (1998), *Status Report on Implementation of ECOWAS Priority Programmes*, ECOWAS Doc. ECW/CMXLIII/13, Abuja: ECOWAS Secretariat.

Fashole D., Shaw T. M. (eds.) (1984), *Continental Crisis: The Lagos Plan of Action and Africa's future*, Lanham, MD: University Press of America.

Francis D. J. (2017), *The Politics of Economic Regionalism. Sierra Leone in ECOWAS*, London and New York: Routledge.

Franck Th. M. (1964), *East African Unity through Law*, New Haven: Yale University Press.

Gandois H. (2014), *Economic Community of West African States*, in L. Levi, G. Finizio, and N. Vallinoto (eds.), *The Democratization of International Institutions. First International Democracy Report*, London and New York: Routledge, pp. 196–206.

Gruhn I. V. (1979), *Regionalism Reconsidered: The Economic Commission for Africa*, Boulder: Westview Press.

Jackson R. H. (1990), *Quasi-States: Sovereignty, International Relations, and the Third World*, Cambridge: Cambridge University Press.

Julienne R. (1967), *The Experience of Integration in French-Speaking Africa*, in A. Hazlewood (ed.), *African Integration and Disintegration: Case Studies in Economic and Political Union*, London: Exford University Press, pp. 339–353.

Kaldor M. (1999), *New and Old Wars: Organized Violence in a Global Era*, Cambridge: Polity Press.

Legum C. (1964), *The Specialized Commissions of the Organisation of African Unity*, in "Journal of Modern African Studies", 2, 4, pp. 587–590.

Makinda S. M., Okumu F. W., Mickler D. (2016), *The African Union. Addressing the Challenges of Peace, Security, and Governance*, London and New York: Routledge.

Malamud A., Gardini G. L. (2012), *Has Regionalism Peaked? The Latin American Quagmire and Its Lessons*, in "International Spectator", 47, 1, pp. 116–133.

Manning P. (1998), *Francophone Sub-Saharian Africa 1880–1995*, Cambridge: Cambridge University Press.

Massell B. F. (1963), *East African Economic Union. An Evaluation and Some Implications for Policy, Memorandum RM-3880-RC*, Santa Monica: Rand Corporation.

Matlosa K. (2007), *South Africa and Regional Security in Southern Africa*, in A. Adebajo, A.Adedeji, and C. Landsberg (eds.), *South Africa in Africa: The Post-Apartheid Era*, Scottsville: University of KwaZulu-Natal Press, pp. 105–126.

Meyer A. (2014a), *Central African Economic and Monetary Community in Central Africa*, in L. Levi, G. Finizio, and N. Vallinoto (eds.), *The Democratization of International Institutions. First International Democracy Report*, London and New York: Routledge, pp. 221–229.

Meyer A. (2014b), *Economic Community of Central African States*, in L. Levi, G. Finizio, and N. Vallinoto (eds.), *The Democratization of International Institutions. First International Democracy Report*, London and New York: Routledge, pp. 215–220.

Meyn M. (2012), *An Anatomy of Economic Partnership Agreements*, in A. Adebajo, K. Whiteman (eds.), *The EU and Africa. From Eurafrique to Afro-Europa*, London: Hurst & Co., pp. 197–216.

Michel L. (2008), *Economic Partnership Agreements: Drivers of Development*, Luxembourg: Office for Official Publications of the European Communities.

Murithi T. (2005), *The African Union: Pan-Africanism, Peacebuilding and Development*, Aldershot: Ashgate.

Murithi T., Ndinga-Muvumba A. (2008), *Building an African Union for the 21st Century*, in J. Akokpari, and A. Ndinga-Muvumba (eds.), *The African Union and Its Institutions*, Auckland Park: Fanele, pp. 1–21.

Nagar D., Ngaje F. (2018), The African Union and Its Relations with Sub-regional Economic Communities, in T. Karbo, and T. Murithi (eds.), *The African Union. Autocracy, Diplomacy and Peacebuilding in Africa*, London: I.B. Tauris, pp. 205–231.

Nkrumah K. (1963), *Africa Must Unite*, London: Heinemann.

Padmore G. (1956), *Pan-Africanism or Communism? The Coming Struggle for Africa*, London: Dobson.

Sanger C. (1964), *Towards Unity in Africa*, in "Foreign Affairs", 42, 2, pp. 269–281.

Sesay A. (1999), *The Limits of Peacekeeping by a Regional Organization: The OAU Peacekeeping Force in Chad*, "Conflict Quarterly", 11, 1, pp. 7–26.

Söderbaum F. (2007), *African Regionalism and EU-African Interregionalism*, in M. Telò (ed.), *European Union and New Regionalism: Regional Actors and Global Governance in a Post-Hegemonic Era*, 2nd ed., Aldershot: Ashgate, pp. 185–202.

Söderbaum F., Hettne B. (2010), *Regional Security in a Global Perspective*, in U. Engel, and J. Gomes Porto (eds.), *Africa's New Security Architecture*, Aldershot: Ashgate, pp. 13–30.

Tavares R., Tang V. (2011), *Regional Economic Integration in Africa: Impediments in Progress?*, in "South African Journal of International Affairs", 18, 2, pp. 217–233.

Telò M. (2014), *Introduction: Globalization, New Regionalism and the Role of the European Union*, in Id. (ed.), *European Union and New Regionalism: Competing Regionalism and Global Governance in a Post-Hegemonic Era*, 3rd ed., London and New York: Routledge, pp. 1–23.

Tevoedjre A. (1965), *Pan-Africanism in Action: An Account of the UAM*, Cambridge (MA): Harvard University Press.

Thompson V. B. (1969), *Africa and Unity: The Evolution of Pan-Africanism*, London: Longman.

Touray O. A. (2016), *The African Union: The First Ten Years*, Lanham: Roman & Littlefield.

UNCTAD (2019), *Key Statistics and Trends in Regional Trade in Africa*, Geneva: United Nations.

Wallerstein I. (1961), *Africa: The Politics of Independence*, New York: Vintage Books (reprinted in Id. *Africa: The Politics of Independence and Unity*, Lincoln: University of Nebraska Press).

Warner C. M. (2001), *The Rise of the State System in Africa*, in "Review of International Studies", 27, 5, pp. 65–89.

Welch Jr. C. E. (1966), *Dreams of Unity: Pan-Africanism and Political Unification in West Africa*, Ithaca: Cornell University Press.

African Continental Free Trade Area: Opportunities and Challenges

ANDREA COFELICE

The *Treaty Establishing the African Continental Free Trade Area* (AfCFTA) adopted at the 10th extraordinary session of the Assembly of Heads of State and Government of the African Union (AU) in March 2018 finally entered into force on May 30, 2019, with the deposit of the 22nd instrument of ratification by Gambia.[1]

In terms of the number of countries involved (with a combined annual GDP that is currently worth over $2tn) and the population concerned (1.2bn), AfCFTA represents the most important free trade agreement since the foundation of the World Trade Organization (WTO). Equally important is the timing of the agreement, as it stands in sharp contrast with an international context marked by a persistent and significant increase in trade-restrictive measures, as well as by a growing resistance (or even hostility) toward the development of regional integration systems.

The establishment of a continental free trade area represents a milestone in a lengthy African integration journey, which should culminate, as envisaged in the 1994 Treaty establishing the African Economic Community (the "Abuja Treaty"), in the creation of a full economic and monetary union by 2028. It is also the first project to be implemented under Agenda 2063, a strategic plan adopted by the AU in 2015 for the socio-economic transformation of the continent in the coming 50 years.[2]

---

[1]   As in September 2019, 54 out of the 55 AU members (with the only exception of Eritrea) have signed the agreement, and 27 states have ratified it.

[2]   Agenda 2063 consists of 12 main objectives including, *inter alia*, the creation of a single African passport and the development of a continentally integrated rail and air transport system.

The main objectives of AfCFTA are certainly ambitious. By removing tariff and non-tariff barriers on goods and services, member states intend to: facilitate intra-African trade; promote regional value chains to foster the integration of the African continent into the global economy; and boost industrialization, competitiveness and innovation, ultimately contributing to Africa's economic development and social progress.

Due to the wide scope of the agreement, negotiations were divided into two phases. The first, which culminated in the March treaty, focused on: phasing out tariffs on 90 % of goods exchanged between African countries; the elimination of non-tariff barriers (i.e., excessively long customs procedures, costly sanitary and phytosanitary measures, complex and heterogeneous rules on product standards and licensing requirements, etc.); the definition of rules of origin; and a deal on customs cooperation and trade remedies. The AfCFTA agreement was also supplemented by the AU *Protocol on Free Movement*, with which the signatory states (currently twenty-seven) grant reciprocal visa waivers, the right of residence and the right of establishment for professional or work reasons to their citizens.

Any decision on the elimination of tariffs related to the remaining 10 % of goods, represented by "sensitive commodities", as well as on other issues such as investments, competition policies and intellectual property rights, was postponed to the second phase of negotiations, launched in July 2019 at the 12th extraordinary summit of the Assembly of the AU held in Niamey.

If evaluated on the basis of classic theories of regional economic integration (Balassa 1973), the AfCFTA would thus exceed the traditional boundaries of "free trade area" models, which are generally limited to removing tariffs and quotas on goods trade. Consistent with the Abuja Treaty, indeed, the AfCFTA agreement already anticipates some of the constitutive elements of a "single market" (namely: abolition of non-tariff barriers, free movement of people and services, investments, intellectual property rights and competition policy) and "economic union" arrangements (by invoking, for instance, the harmonization of regulatory policies).

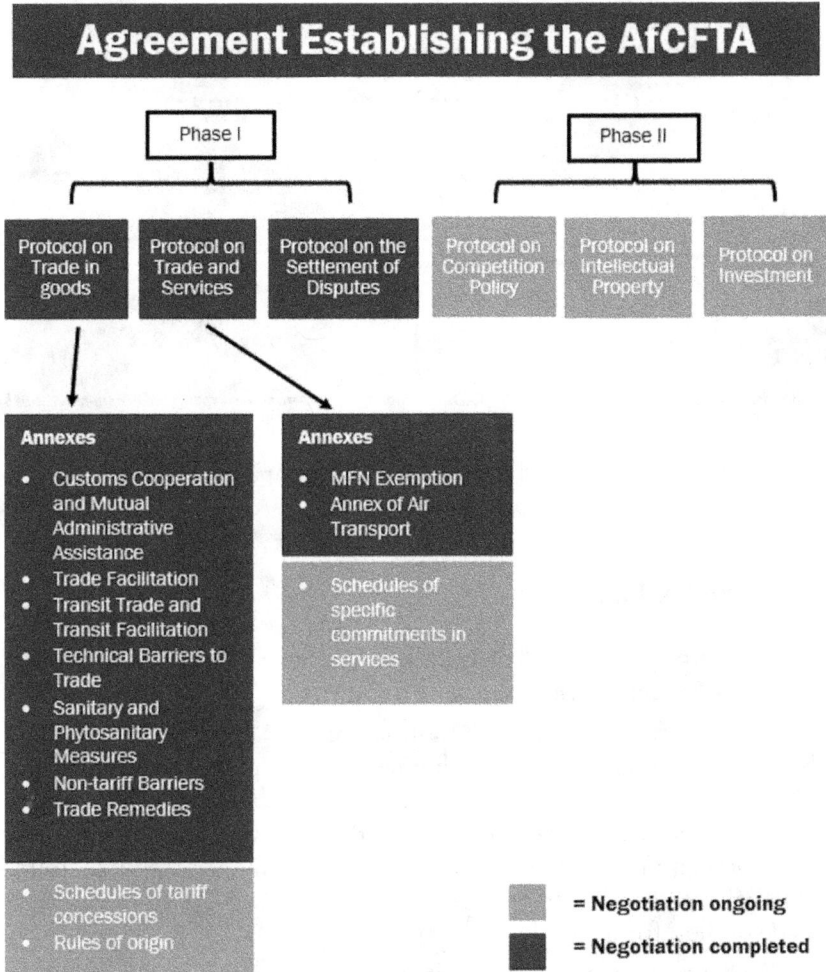

Agreement Establishing the AfCFTA

Phase I

- Protocol on Trade in goods
- Protocol on Trade and Services
- Protocol on the Settlement of Disputes

Phase II

- Protocol on Competition Policy
- Protocol on Intellectual Property
- Protocol on Investment

Annexes

- Customs Cooperation and Mutual Administrative Assistance
- Trade Facilitation
- Transit Trade and Transit Facilitation
- Technical Barriers to Trade
- Sanitary and Phytosanitary Measures
- Non-tariff Barriers
- Trade Remedies

- Schedules of tariff concessions
- Rules of origin

Annexes

- MFN Exemption
- Annex of Air Transport

- Schedules of specific commitments in services

☐ = Negotiation ongoing

■ = Negotiation completed

Fig. 1: Status of AfCFTA protocols and annexes.
Source: Signé and van der Ven (2019, p. 3).

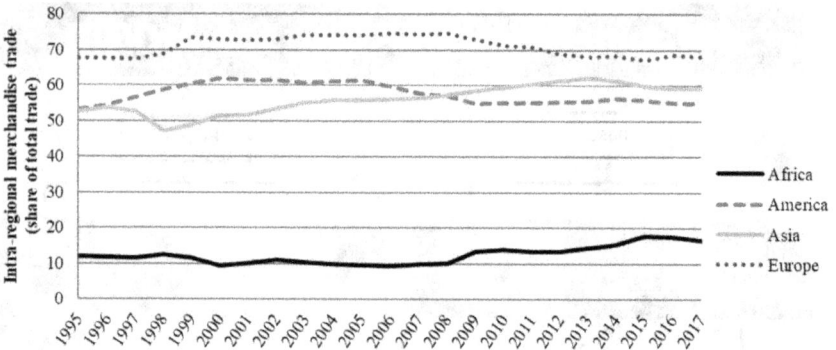

Source: Author's elaboration based on UNCTAD, *Merchandise: Intra-trade and extra-trade of country groups by product, annual*, 2017, at: https://unctadstat.unctad.org

Fig. 2: Africa's intra-regional merchandise trade compared to other regional blocs.

1. Expected Benefits

The importance of this agreement becomes immediately clear if compared to the current trends in African trade.

High tariffs, inadequate infrastructure and excessive bureaucratic burdens, especially at national borders, represent the main structural obstacles which have so far hampered the development of a fully fledged intra-African market. Indeed, the United Nations Conference on Trade and Development (UNCTAD) reports that in 2017 Africa's intra-regional merchandise trade accounted for a mere 16.6 % of the total trade of the African continent.[3]

Furthermore, most of this trade still occurs *within* regional economic communities, often between neighboring countries.

"Internal" structural weaknesses have also led to a growing marginalization of the African continent in global trade relations. Although over 80 % of African trade is oriented toward Europe, Asia and America, Africa's share of world exports remains not only extremely modest (accounting for less than 3 % of world exports in 2017), but it is also tied to extractive raw materials, agricultural and food products (in

---

[3]   https://unctadstat.unctad.org (latest access: September 2019).

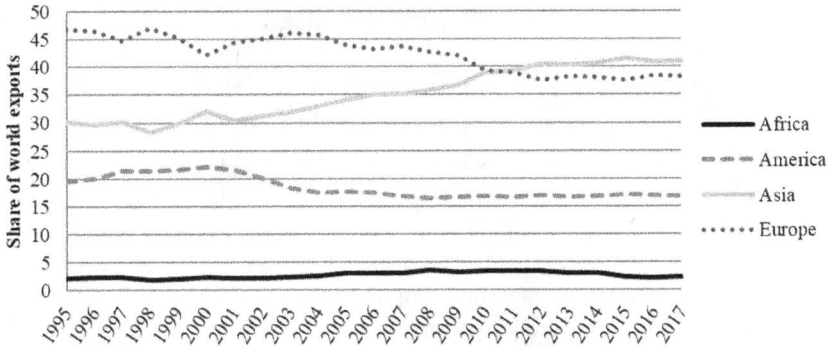

Source: Author's elaboration based on UNCTAD. *Merchandise: Total trade and share, annual,* 2017. at: https://unctadstat.unctad.org

Fig. 3: Africa's share of world exports compared to other regional blocs.

2017, manufactured goods accounted only for about 15 % of Africa's extra-regional exports).[4] Since the 1980s, there has been a constant decrease in African production and exports, in terms of both volume, variety and added value. In contrast, Africa's imports are predominantly characterized by manufactured and industrial goods (which represent, for instance, 70 % of Africa's total imports from Europe).

The current inherited, traditional over-reliance in raw materials has therefore placed the African continent in a long-term disadvantaged position, in terms of both commercial losses (in cumulative terms) and the under-development of productive and growth capacities.

Against this background, what are the benefits expected from AfCFTA implementation?

According to the UN Economic Commission for Africa,[5] the implementation of the agreement could, by 2022, increase intra-African trade by 52 % (compared to 2010 levels) thus reducing the gap with intra-regional trade quotas currently characterizing Asia, America and Europe (see Fig. 2 above). In the short term, the main beneficiaries of AfCFTA would be small- and medium-sized enterprises that today account for 80 % of the continent's companies. However, in the medium

---

[4] https://unctadstat.unctad.org (latest access: September 2019).

[5] See https://www.uneca.org/afcfta-business-summit-2018 (latest access: September 2019).

to long term, the benefits will extend to all African citizens, who will achieve a welfare gain estimated at $16.1bn, especially favoring women (who currently manage 70 % of informal cross-border trade) and young people, who could benefit from new job opportunities.

Intra-African economic and commercial growth would mainly affect the industrial and manufacturing sectors, thus demonstrating AfCFTA's potential role in guiding the structural transformation of African countries. Indeed, as already mentioned, Africa's extra-regional trade, tied as it is to exports of raw materials and agricultural products, is not in itself capable of adequately supporting the continental industrialization process. On the contrary, since Africa's intra-regional trade is relatively more diversified and with greater added value (in 2017, manufactured goods represented over 40 % of Africa's intra-regional trade),[6] it offers greater opportunities for industrial development and revitalization.

The goal of promoting rapid African industrialization involves complex challenges, including the development of adequate continental infrastructure. In this specific field, the reference strategy is the 2010 *Programme for infrastructure development in Africa*, which is a promising example of how regional integration goals, business strategies and infrastructure investments can be coordinated and pursued simultaneously with a view to meeting Africa's infrastructure needs in key sectors such as energy (especially clean and renewable energy), information and communication technologies, and transboundary transport and water resources.

At the same time, African countries cannot realistically hope to improve the living conditions of their peoples and reduce widespread poverty without adopting effective measures aiming at boosting the development of the agricultural sector. In the short and medium term, agriculture is, and will continue to be, one of the main sources of income, employment and foreign currency receipts: African countries should thus create the necessary linkages between agriculture and other sectors of their economies.

Such "internal" progress could, in turn, contribute to strengthening Africa's position in global trade. With the failure of the Doha Round and the crisis of multilateral trade negotiations (and ultimately of the WTO's ruling authority), the latest international trade rules have been

---

[6]   https://unctadstat.unctad.org (latest access: September 2019).

fixed under preferential agreements negotiated at bilateral, regional (i.e. continental) or trans-regional levels, from which Africa has been almost systematically excluded. The consolidation of African regionalism might therefore prove pivotal: on the one hand, in developing an adequate negotiating power *vis-à-vis* relevant commercial partners (such as the EU and China), and on the other, in promoting economies of scale and value chains that can improve African companies' ability to compete on international markets.

The realization of these benefits, however, is conditional on the overcoming of numerous political, legal, economic and functional challenges.

2. Challenges and Obstacles to AfCFTA Implementation

2.1 Adopting a win-win approach

At the top of political priorities, there is the need to bring into the agreement those countries that have still not ratified it (i.e., half of the AU members), paying specific attention to Nigeria, since it represents, along with South Africa and Egypt, the main economic driving forces of the continent.[7] In particular, there are two issues that currently hamper the accession process: the concern that the elimination of tariffs could put the survival of national production at risk; and the issue of compensation for those countries that rely on customs duties to consolidate their (fragile) national budgets.

It is true that, at the aggregate level, the introduction of AfCFTA would result in a relatively modest economic shock, not only because of the low volume of Africa's intra-regional trade, but also because, according to UNCTAD, revenue losses due to tariff removals (estimated in a total of \$4.1bn) will be offset by a general increase in revenue from trade taxes, due to the expansion of Africa's intra-regional trade (UNCTAD 2015).

However, empirical evidence shows that free trade agreements can lead to: the demise of uncompetitive industries and services; significant adjustment costs for some vulnerable groups (such as small-scale

---

[7]   These three countries alone contribute over 50 % of Africa's cumulative GDP: in this sense, the AfCFTA would have the greatest levels of income disparity of any continental free trade agreement (Akeyewale 2018).

producers, informal traders, etc.) as well as for those countries (especially least developed and landlocked countries) that depend chiefly upon import duties for their public revenues; and, more generally, an uneven distribution of costs and benefits between countries with dissimilar development rates and resource capacities (a particularly sensitive problem in Africa, where seven countries alone account for about 60 % of total intra-African merchandise exports (UNCTAD 2015).

It is therefore necessary to adopt cohesion policies and *ad hoc* measures to support the specific needs of different types of countries and national actors, in order to make AfCFTA an inclusive and mutually beneficial agreement for all. This is not only a matter of equity, but also of effectiveness: it has been proven, indeed, that commercial agreements that are not advantageous for all the parties involved tend to either remain on paper or deteriorate over time, precisely because the parties have little interest in their application.

These policies could be built upon three pillars: the creation of an adjustment and compensation fund; the promotion of capacity building programs; and the organization of systematic consultation with economic and non-state actors.

The implementation of AfCFTA should first of all go hand in hand with the creation of an adjustment and compensation fund for those countries that will be negatively affected by the structural and regulatory changes introduced by the agreement. The importance of this fund is confirmed by the fact that tax administration systems of many African states are still weak and continue to depend upon import duties. For this group of countries, a well-funded compensation fund, with clear eligibility criteria and rapid payment procedures, would permit the minimization of possible drawbacks while implementing the necessary reforms to adapt their domestic system to AfCFTA. It would also produce additional benefits over time, in terms of increased competitiveness and a reduction of the need for international financial assistance, thus avoiding the emergence of a costly and inefficient system of interminable international subsidies.

After all, a number of African regional economic communities already provide financial compensation schemes, including mechanisms for sharing the benefits deriving from trade liberalization among member states. For instance, the Economic Community of West African States (ECOWAS) established a *Fund for Cooperation, Compensation and*

Development (more recently transformed into ECOWAS Bank for Investment and Development) in order to compensate member states for any losses incurred as a result of Community liberalization processes. The Southern African Customs Union (SACU) has instead adopted an Agreement detailing the *Revenue Sharing Formula* that is used for determining each member state's share out of all customs, excise and additional duties collected in the common customs area. This formula also embraces a "development component", which is currently fixed at 15 % of total excise revenue and is distributed according to the inverse of each country's GDP per capita, thus aiming to compensate the least developed economies.

Secondly, the implementation of AfCFTA should be accompanied by capacity building programs to ensure that all African countries and stakeholders are fully aware of AfCFTA objectives, rules and mechanisms, and are able to exploit its benefits and opportunities.

These programs should have a twofold purpose. Firstly, they should assist (mostly small- and medium-sized) businessmen and firms to orient their production toward intra-African trade. To this end, AfCFTA institutions and member states should invest in economic and trade training services (with a specific focus on the most complex issues of the agreement, such as rules of origin and trade remedies) and facilitate initial access to financing. Secondly, they should both empower specific categories of beneficiaries (e.g. youth and women) and protect vulnerable groups who may suffer from trade liberalization (e.g. informal cross-border traders and rural food producers). Adequate forms of protection for these groups might include exclusion clauses and safeguard measures. Although discussion on these latter topics has been postponed to phase II, it will be important to ensure that any safeguard mechanism be sufficiently accessible for less developed economies and for the most vulnerable social groups, while simultaneously providing careful monitoring to assess the impact of these measures.

Finally, the development of standing consultation mechanisms with private sector and civil society organizations will be a key factor for the success of AfCFTA.

Here, tools such as the *Country Business Index*, which will soon be launched by the UN Economic Commission for Africa, and the *Afrobarometer*, will be useful for monitoring, at continental level, the perceptions of economic operators and the general public respectively, in relation to the actual impact of the agreement. In addition, member states should set up, at the national level, adequate mechanisms to periodically consult interested stakeholders and ensure that their opinions are fully considered. A particular role in this sense could be played by parliaments, which could set up institutional forums to involve producers and agricultural associations, consumer organizations, chambers of commerce and industry, media, civil society groups (especially those dealing with workers' rights, environment, gender and youth issues) and the academic community.

2.2 Setting Up Law-Based Governance with a Multi-Level Institutional Design

After obtaining the necessary political support at the highest decision-making levels, the main objective will be to define AfCFTA technically and ensure its effective implementation. Historically, indeed, one of the main obstacles to regional integration in Africa has not so much been a lack of farsighted strategies or ambitious policies, but in their actual implementation.

Accordingly, AfCFTA's success will largely depend on the establishment of an appropriate governance system, based on the rule of law and on a solid institutional architecture, to promote, as requested by the African Development Bank (2014), harmonization, consistency and predictability goals.

During negotiations, two alternative institutional models were discussed. One option discussed was the possibility of "hosting" AfCFTA bodies within the AU institutional framework by setting up, for instance, a specific department within the AU Commission. Alternatively, member states were tempted to establish a brand new international intergovernmental organization, (a WTO-like "African Trade Organization"), totally detached from the AU: the risk, however, was to create an unnecessary and expensive institutional duplication of the AU, with related problems of coordination and division of labor between the two organizations.

The final decision represents a sort of compromise between these two initial alternatives. The agreement, indeed, provides for the establishment of an AfCFTA Secretariat, with a legal personality distinct from that of the AU, but governed by the political bodies of the Union, namely the

Assembly of the AU (composed of the Heads of State and government of member states) and the Executive council (composed of African trade ministers), supported by a Committee of senior trade officials.

As far as the AfCFTA Secretariat is concerned, its composition, budget and functions are currently being defined by the Assembly of the Union and the Council of Ministers.[8] Regardless of its final configuration and legal status, it is crucial that the Secretariat perform not only administrative functions, but also executive ones, including: the coordination of AfCFTA policies implementation; monitoring and evaluation; technical assistance; and consultation and communication with member states and non-state actors. It is possible, yet, that in the medium/long term the AU Commission will be reorganized and equipped with additional resources to serve as the AfCFTA Secretariat, too.

In order to prevent a repetition of examples of past poor performance, setting up a monitoring system to assess progress toward the implementation of AfCFTA's commitments should be one of the core functions of the future Secretariat. In this sense, a tool such as the *Single Market Scoreboard*, used by the EU Commission to evaluate the level of transposition of EU law into national law in an accurate and timely fashion, can be a useful reference model, with a view to exerting pressure on member states to accelerate the implementation of regional commitments.

At least two critical remarks can be made about the agreed institutional setup. By largely relying on the institutional umbrella of the AU, AfCFTA will indeed also import its main decision-making mechanism, i.e., the rule of consensus among its member states, with predictable consequences for the effectiveness of deliberative processes (whose limits are already known in the context of the AU). Secondly, the agreement does not assign an institutional role for the Pan-African Parliament within AfCFTA. Admittedly, this body does not have significant legislative powers; nevertheless, it could perform important functions of an advisory (acting as a permanent forum for dialogue and argument between institutional, economic and civil society actors) and monitoring nature: not so much of the AfCFTA's economic impact (which falls under the responsibility

---

[8] During its 12th Extraordinary Sessions held in July 2019, the Assembly of the AU, after announcing the location of the AfCFTA Secretariat (Republic of Ghana), decided that it shall be operational by the first quarter of 2020 (Doc. Ext/Assembly/ AU/ Dec.2(XII)).

of the Secretariat), as of its consequences in terms of social and human rights.

AfCFTA's institutional design should also adopt a multi-level perspective and be supported by (sub-)regional and national institutions.

In particular, at the (sub-)regional level, the main challenge will be to rationalize and harmonize the different (and sometimes conflicting) regimes of African regional economic communities (RECs) *vis-à-vis* the aims and timing set for AfCFTA's functioning. The African continent is currently marked by the presence of 18 preferential trade agreements: a so-called *spaghetti bowl* composed of economic, monetary and sectoral cooperation agreements, presenting a thorny problem of overlap, duplication and unavoidable competition among themselves. Among these (sub-)regional groups, the AU recognizes eight RECs as building blocks of the continental integration process.[9]

While the very existence of RECs reveals African countries' genuine interest in promoting regional integration as a development strategy, it must be acknowledged that the results achieved so far have not always met expectations: empirical evidence reflects a very patchy situation across the African continent, in terms of actual economic, political and institutional integration.[10]

In spite of this, RECs are called on to play a key role in ensuring the effective implementation and harmonization of many of AfCFTA's substantial issues, through the setting up of steering committees and technical working groups operating under the supervision and coordination of continental institutions. A first step in this direction was constituted by the launch of the first *Mid-Year Coordination meeting of the African Union and the Regional Economic Communities* last July with a view to aligning their respective work programs, coordinating the implementation of the continental integration agenda and mapping out

---

[9]   Arab Maghreb Union (AMU); Economic Community of West African States (ECOWAS); East African Community (EAC); Intergovernmental Authority on Development (IGAD); Southern African Development Community (SADC); Common Market for Eastern and Southern Africa (COMESA); Economic Community of Central African States (ECCAS); and Community of Sahel-Saharan States (CENSAD).

[10]   See, in this sense, data from the *Africa Regional Integration Index*, at https://www.integrate-africa.org/

a clearer division of labor and effective collaboration between the AU and RECs.[11]

While waiting for continental and (sub-)regional institutions to become operational, the most immediate step consisted in the creation, by each member state, of *ad hoc* ministerial agencies in charge of the implementation of all AfCFTA-related matters at the national level. After all, this kind of scheme is already used (with some success) in a number of RECs, especially in the East African Community (EAC). Here, member states have established a distinct government agency, with a mandate to coordinate the implementation of Community commitments at the national level, as well as to promote the adaptation of national legislation to Community norms.

Finally, in order to give greater legal certainty and predictability to the agreement's obligations, AfCFTA's institutional framework is completed by a dispute settlement mechanism, which is mandatory and binding for member states. This mechanism, which is clearly based on the WTO model, provides that each state can turn to a *Dispute settlement body*, which is organized in panels (a sort of first-degree chambers) and in an appellate body, to challenge other states' application or interpretation of AfCFTA rules.

Drawing on practices already adopted in some RECs, especially in the Common Market of East and South Africa (COMESA), the Dispute settlement body will initially facilitate direct negotiations between involved states; in case of their failure, non-contentious instruments will be proposed, such as mediation and conciliation, before resorting to contentious litigation.

In addition to this mechanism, which is exclusively intergovernmental, it would be appropriate to explicitly recognize the possibility for individuals to assert their rights under AfCFTA. In this sense, the juridical framework should be developed according to a subsidiarity principle.

National courts represent the first institutional level to which citizens, private companies and other non-state actors could turn to obtain adequate remedies for alleged violations of their rights deriving from

---

[11] The launch of the Mid-Year Coordination meeting with RECs is part of the broader reform process of the AU. The Assembly of the AU, instead of holding two yearly summits from now on, will gather only once a year: its mid-year summit has indeed been replaced by the Coordination Meeting with RECs.

AfCFTA obligations. Secondly, a tiered system of complaints and appeals should be envisaged, involving national courts, RECs courts (where existing) and, as a last resort, the African Court on Human and Peoples' Rights,[12] which should be equipped with an *ad hoc* "trade chamber", also with a view to create positive synergies between trade law and human rights law.

2.3 Strengthening the interlinkage between human rights and trade liberalization

Although the promotion of human rights does not represent AfCFTA's core interest, a close linkage exists between the enhancement of human rights and one of the fundamental objectives of the continental free trade area: improving the living conditions of African people. The number of jobs that could be created through the growth of intra-African trade has the potential to significantly promote, in the medium-long term, social and economic rights and poverty reduction.

In the short term, however, trade liberalization and economic integration might not automatically lead to fair and sustainable outcomes. Trade liberalization can produce uneven impacts on various socio-economic groups, due to their different access to goods, credit and economic opportunities, training and specialization, and employment. Agricultural trade liberalization, for instance, is a particularly sensitive issue, due to its potentially negative impact on African people's food security.

Assessing the distributional impact of the AfCFTA agreement is thus crucial to ensure the complementarity between human rights promotion and trade liberalization. As acknowledged by the World Bank (2012), human rights approaches tend to improve development outcomes and the quality of economic growth, by mainstreaming distributional issues and identifying safety net measures during phases of economic adjustment. Human rights approaches not only offer procedural tools,

---

[12]   In the near future, this Court will be replaced by the African Court of Justice and Human Rights, whose founding Protocol was adopted in July 2008 by the Assembly of the African Union and will come into force after reaching the 15th ratification instrument. To date, six African states have ratified the Protocol: Benin, Burkina Faso, Congo, Libya, Liberia and Mali.

but also define the normative framework to assess the impact of new policies and economic measures.[13]

Such an assessment is even more relevant in light of a general and growing skepticism toward trade liberalization processes, fueled to a large extent by a widespread perception that the benefits of trade and globalization have not been equally distributed. It is therefore necessary to adopt appropriate policies to ensure that the potential benefits in terms of increased productivity and welfare deriving from the realization of AfCFTA are equally distributed.

In order to make AfCFTA a socially sustainable and inclusive agreement, in addition to the cohesion and adjustment policies and the mechanisms for consultation and access to remedies already analyzed above, it would also be appropriate to: adopt a gradual and targeted approach to liberalization processes; monitor the impact of the agreement on the economic and social rights of the populations involved; and maintain political control over the implementation of the agreement.

A gradual and targeted approach to liberalization processes would allow for the most vulnerable groups of the population to be protected, especially in vital sectors such as food security. In this sense, the introduction of "exclusion lists", on which discussion was postponed to the second phase of AfCFTA negotiation, represents a key tool, allowing governments to select a certain number of sensitive items to be temporarily excluded from tariff liberalization. The selection of these items should pursue the primary goal of protecting vulnerable groups and mitigating the negative impact of tariff liberalization on customs revenue.

For this purpose, a relevant landmark is represented by the list of strategic agricultural commodities that African countries have pledged to promote and protect, which was adopted at the 2006 Abuja Food Security Summit and includes: rice, legumes, maize, cotton, oil palm, beef, dairy, poultry and fisheries products at the continental level; and cassava, sorghum and millet at (sub-)regional level.[14] These commodities

---

[13] The African human rights legal and political framework is mainly defined by the *African Charter on Human and Peoples Rights* and *Agenda 2063: The Africa We Want*, as well as by the major UN human rights treaties ratified by African countries.

[14] See: *Decision on the Summit on Food Security in Africa*, Abuja, Nigeria, 4–7 December 2006, doc. Assembly/AU/6(VIII).

have been defined "of strategic importance" due to their significance in the African food basket, their contribution to overall continental export earnings or import bills, and their unexploited production, value-addition and trade potential for the African continent.

Additionally, it will be necessary to include, among the AfCFTA's monitoring tools, a mechanism to assess the distributional and human rights impacts of the free trade agreement. Giving a mandate to the Pan-African Parliament, or one of the AU human rights related bodies, to launch regular and systematic human rights impact assessments would represent one of the viable options to be explored, to identify the compensatory, adjustment or accompanying measures that may be necessary so that the AfCFTA continues to meet the economic, social and development needs of the continent over time.

Finally, human rights law requires institutions to adopt legislative, administrative, budgetary, judicial and other measures that are "appropriate" to protect and promote human rights. But what is "appropriate" may change over time and with changing circumstances. Economic development is indeed a dynamic process: therefore, African institutions should be very careful not to limit their political room for maneuver for the future. In other words, they should abstain from including, in the technical and operational agreements that will be adopted at the end of the second phase of AfCFTA negotiations, any provision that could undermine the institutional capacity to ensure that human rights are effectively protected and respected in the future.

2.4 Diversifying financial sources

However, a caveat remains: without strategic investments and funding supporting its setting-up and organization, the grand vision of a continental free trade area will just remain wishful thinking.

The role of international donors will thus be crucial: The World Bank and the EU have widely expressed their willingness to contribute to the necessary funds for the implementation of the agreement. The EU, in particular, has already begun to financially support AfCFTA, both directly, through the *Pan-African Programme*,[15] under the Joint

---

[15]   As in June 2019, the EU had already committed Eur 62.5 million to support the launch of six AfCFTA-related projects. Data can be retrieved from https://ec.europa.

Africa–EU Strategy (2014–2020), and indirectly through the *Africa-Europe Alliance for Sustainable Investment and Jobs*, launched by former Commission President Juncker in September 2018 as part of the EU External Investment Plan (2017–2020),[16] which is expected to unlock sustainable private and public-sector investment to foster trade and job creation (i.e. the two main AfCFTA's objectives).

Additional financial support should be provided by Africa-based international organizations, such as the African Development Bank, the UN Economic Commission for Africa and UNCTAD, and by *aid for trade initiatives* run by the WTO and the OECD, among others. Pending the establishment of the AfCFTA Secretariat, the AU Commission could convene a donor conference and coordinate the implementation of financial commitments through the establishment of a joint steering committee.

Looking ahead, however, funding for the AfCFTA budget will have to increasingly rely on the mobilization of continental public and private resources. But before postulating a system of own resources, African governments should first commit themselves to improving and rationalizing national public revenues, by making tax systems more equitable, transparent and effective, and by resolutely addressing chronic corruption problems, weak institutional capacities, restricted tax bases, and pervasive tax avoidance and evasion.

This is the only way that the chronic dependence of African development projects on foreign aid, and the connected risk of replicating initiatives run by donors rather than by African stakeholders, can be finally overcome, providing local actors with greater control and responsibility vis-à-vis their own political choices.

3. Conclusions

It is clear from the above analysis that the main challenges to the realization of an African free trade area are intrinsically political rather than economic in nature. AfCFTA represents a window of opportunity

---

eu/europeaid/regions/africa/continental-cooperation/pan-african-programme_en

[16] Under this plan, total expected investments by 2020 are Eur 44 billion (with Eur 37.1 billion already in motion as at June 2019). Data can be retrieved from: https://ec.europa.eu/commission/africaeuropealliance_en

for African countries to promote intra-African trade, diversify and structurally transform the continent's economy, and pursue important human rights and anti-poverty goals set in Agenda 2063 (which the AfCFTA is part of). In this sense, far from being antithetical, regional integration and human rights are interdependent and, through legal commitments and the setting-up of regional institutions in charge of their implementation, jointly contribute to defining the purpose and functions of sovereignty in Africa.

However, the harmonization of national priorities to achieve regional and global public goods will require firm political will, determination and coordinating efforts by African political leaders.

What are the next steps? The 2018 AfCFTA agreement outlines only its legal framework.

During the current second phase of negotiations, which is expected to lead to the dismantling of tariffs by July 2020,[17] particularly sensitive issues have to be discussed, including: sources of funding and investments; compensation mechanisms; and the definition of "sensitive commodities" to be exempted from the abolition of tariffs. In the meantime, the Secretariat is expected to be established in order to manage the operational phase of the agreement.

The above choices and decisions will determine the chance to shape a cohesive regional bloc, which can contribute to Africa's economic and social development and its integration in the global economy.

References

African Development Bank (2014), *African Development Report 2014. Regional Integration for Inclusive Growth*, at www.afdb.org/en/documents/document/african-development-report-2014-leveraging-regional-integration-for-inclusive-growth-50901 (accessed September 2019).

Akeyewale R. (2018), *Who Are the Winners and Losers of the AfCFTA*, World Economic Forum, 17 October 2018, at www.weforum.org/agenda/2018/10/africa-continental-free-trade-afcfta-sme-business (accessed September 2019).

---

[17] See: *Decision on the Launch of the Operational Phase of the African Continental Free Trade Area*, 12th Extraordinary Session of the Assembly of the AU, 7 July 2019, Niamey (Niger), doc. Ext/Assembly/AU/ Dec.1(XII).

Balassa B. (1973), *The Theory of Economic Integration*, London: Allen and Unwin.

Signé L. and van der Ven C. (2019), *Keys to Success for the AfCFTA Negotiations*, Washington, DC: Brookings Institution Policy Brief.

UNCTAD (2015), *The Continental Free Trade Area: Making It Work for Africa*, Policy Brief No. 44, December 2015.

UN Economic Commission for Africa (2017), *Assessing Regional Integration in Africa VIII: Bringing the Continental Free Trade Area About*, Addis Ababa: ECA Printing and Publishing Unit.

World Bank (2012), *Human Rights and Economics: Tensions and Positive Relationships*, at www.worldbank.org/en/programs/nordic-trust-fund#2 (accessed September 2019).

A Green New Deal for Europe and Africa

Alberto Majocchi

1. Europe and Africa: Developing a New Partnership

Since the end of the Cold War, the attention of the two traditional Superpowers toward the economic and political development of the African Continent has weakened. There has, however, been an increasing involvement of the new Chinese Superpower, but with a neo-colonial approach: exploitation of mineral and natural resources paid with investments mainly in the transport network in order to facilitate the penetration of Chinese goods in domestic African markets. In this period, Europe has been practically absent, except in some local disputes, with its policy accomplished prevailingly through bilateral relationships.

Things have changed radically with the explosion of the problem of migration that has become one of the main sources of political dispute inside European countries. This problem concerns not only flows from African countries, but also from the Middle East region and from some countries in Asia. But the main flow of migrants comes from the Mediterranean and Sub-Saharan area, with people moving through the desert and arriving at the coast, where they try to find a boat to reach the European coast.

The second reason for Europe's increased interest in the future of Africa is related to energy. Concerns about the issue of climate change, and difficult relationships with oil-producing countries, have forced the European Union to design a policy for progressively curbing the use of fossil fuels and promoting the exploitation of renewable resources. The Sahara Desert is hence being seen as an inexhaustible source of solar energy, but its exploitation requires technological innovation and a massive flow of investment, and an engagement in promoting security and political stability in the region.

Thus, the future of the European Union appears more and more linked to the growth – economic and political – of African countries, with a new approach that envisages a policy of close partnership between the two Continents. This new policy requires many steps forward by Europe, but a new approach by African countries as well.

2. The Control of Migration

To contextualize the problem of controlling the flow of migrants into the European territory, a short analysis of the current conditions of the sub-Saharan economies is needed. Starting in the mid-1990s, and for about 20 years, the majority of sub-Saharan countries recorded high economic growth. But since 2015, increases in income have slowed, in particular for resource-intensive countries, mainly due to the adverse terms-of-trade shock of 2014, as oil exporters have faced the largest real oil price decline since 1970. For non-resource-intensive countries, growth has been more or less in line with the forecasts. Nevertheless, overall, "by 2023 more than half of sub-Saharan African countries won't see a narrowing in their per capita income gap with the rest of the world. And these countries are home to more than two-thirds of the region's total population."[1] Furthermore, while in this context it appears more and more difficult to generate jobs for some 20m new entrants into the labor market every year, it must be considered that some 40 percent of people in sub-Saharan Africa live on less than US$1.25 a day.

This is the reality that Europe has to consider in order to set up a fair and efficient policy to manage movements of migrants, combining solidarity with a rational control of these flows. In the first place, it must be recognized that these flows will continue and no attempt to stop these movements can be effective. The only way out will be to promote a *European Growth Plan with Africa*, capable of combining the future needs of the European economy with a perspective of real growth for African countries.

---

[1]   IMF, *Sub-Saharan Africa. Recovery Amid Elevated Uncertainty*, April 2019.

3. Intra- and Extra-Continental African Migration

Even if the public attention is mainly concentrated on migration from Africa to Europe, it must be recognized that in recent decades the greater part of migration flows has taken place within the Continent. In 1960, total migrations from Africa to the rest of the world amounted to 1.830.776, while migrations within Africa were equal to 6.176.385. In the year 2000, the relative share of extra-continental migrations increased to 8.734.478, but domestic – within Africa – migrations were still higher (10.500.000).[2] It is only recently that the rate of increase of extra-continental migrations has briskly risen. So, for instance, "the emigration growth rate for sub-Saharan Africa during the 1990s stood at just 1 %, before climbing rapidly to 25 % in the 2000s and 31 % in the 2000–2017 period".[3]

This phenomenon is commonly explained by remarking that emigration rates tend to increase as poor countries develop, before falling as they reach middle-income status. This means that growth is necessary, but not solely sufficient condition for the control of migration flows in the short run. As a matter of fact, African countries with higher rates of per capita growth show higher levels of extra-continental migration, while poorer countries tend to have lower levels of extra-continental migration, while their migration is mainly directed toward other African countries.

These facts should be kept in mind in designing a European policy for controlling migration flows. A European effort to support growth in the African Continent is an absolute necessity but can only succeed in the medium term. In parallel, Europe should pursue a foreign and security policy capable of safeguarding and controlling migration flows that will ensure the respect of safety and human dignity of migrants, in countries of origin, in transit and on arrival. This policy will require a similar effort in African countries to put in place the right conditions for promoting an increase in per capita income. This is a task at a continental scale: the size of each national state is insufficient to support an effective development plan. The recent decision to create an African Continental

---

[2]   Flahaux M.L. and De Haas H., "African migration: trends, patterns, drivers", *Comparative Migration Studies*, 2016, 4:1.

[3]   Mallett R., "Exploring Intra- and Extra-Continental African Migration: Trends, Drivers and Policy Options", in Carbone G. (ed.), *A Vision of Africa's Future. Mapping Change, Transformations and Trajectories Towards 2030*, ISPI, Milano, 2018, p.151.

Free Trade Area is important from this point of view as well, since it could support endogenous growth that will redirect migration flows within the Continent, in so far as increased regional trade flows promote higher levels of per capita incomes.

4. Previous Proposals for Controlling migration

In an important contribution to shaping an EU strategy on migration,[4] a former Italian government emphasized that the goal for all existing initiatives and instruments in the field of external action should be to develop an active strategy, focusing first and foremost on the African countries of origin and transit of such migrants. In describing the relevant instruments for this action, the Italian non-paper suggested that investment projects of high social and infrastructural impact should be jointly identified with African partner countries as a crucial incentive for enhancing cooperation with the EU.

In the same perspective, on 14 September 2016, the European Commission proposed an ambitious *External Investment Plan*[5] to support investment in partner countries in Africa (and the European Neighborhood) to promote a new model for participation by the private sector and to help achieve the Sustainable Development Goals, adopted by the United Nations on September 2015. This external action is conceived in the same spirit as the Juncker Plan, through the creation of a new *European Fund for Sustainable Development* (EFSD), which is expected to trigger additional public and private investment volumes, providing partial guarantees to intermediary financing institutions that will, in turn, provide support via loans, guarantees, equity or similar products, to end beneficiaries. In this way, the EFSD could mobilize total investments up to €44bn, based on a €3.35bn contribution from the EU budget and the European Development Fund. If Member States fully

---

[4]   Italian Non-Paper, *Migration Compact. Contribution to an EU strategy for external action on migration,* April 2016.

[5]   European Commission, *Strengthening European investments for jobs and growth. Towards a second phase of the European Fund for Strategic Investments and a new European External Investment Plan,* Brussels, COM/2016/0581.

match the European contribution, the initiative could mobilize more than €88bn in additional investment.

These proposals should create a check on the flow of migrants moving from African countries to Europe, particularly in the case of economic migrants mainly originating from Sub-Saharan countries, where the global economic crisis has resulted in a further deterioration of living conditions.

5. Economic Migrants and Refugees

Empirically, a clear distinction should be drawn between economic migrants and refugees. The first are fleeing poverty and the lack of more favorable economic perspectives; the second fear for their lives in the face of wars, domestic conflicts or oppressive political regimes. The problem of economic migrants requires a growth plan capable of improving economic conditions in countries of origin or transit. The problem of refugees requires a European foreign policy, firstly able to solve the problems of the Middle East, where the conflict between Israel and the Palestinians is permanent, and the new conflicts that began in Iraq, then in Syria, and the long-running domestic war in Yemen. All these circumstances can promote religious fanaticism and feed terrorism, while oppressive political regimes make it difficult for supporters of democracy to survive in these countries. But it is also the case in many African countries that political instability and domestic conflicts bring about large flows of refugees.

The problem in this case is that the European Union is incapable of promptly taking the necessary decisions, given the weakness of European governance: the current rule in this area of competency is unanimity and, even when the prevailing view requires European intervention in order to solve these conflicts, the veto of one member state holds back the launch of a common policy. This has been, *inter alia,* the case with Libya, where the absence of a powerful government has created conditions of anarchy which favors rule by different tribal leaders. Recently, in the speech presented at the European Parliament for her appointment as President of the European Commission, Ursula von der Leyen proposed that in some cases a majority vote could be used for taking decisions on foreign and security policy. This is a first step to open the way toward an efficient European policy in this area.

6. Growth in African Countries

The problem of economic migration is strictly linked to growth prospects of African countries. Between 2010 and 2015, African GDP grew by 3.3 % a year, a sharp decline from the 5.4 % average annual growth rate achieved between 2000 and 2010. But these global figures[6] misrepresent the real situation, since the overall slowdown in Africa's growth was largely determined by what happened during this period of time in the North African countries caught up in the turmoil of the Arab Spring and in oil exporting countries affected by the sharp drop in oil prices.

In the Arab Spring countries (Egypt, Libya and Tunisia, representing 18 % of African GDP) real annual growth rate in 2015 was zero (compared to 4.8 % between 2000 and 2010); in oil exporting countries (Algeria, Angola, Chad, Democratic Republic of Congo, Equatorial Guinea, Gabon, Nigeria and Sudan, representing 40 % of African GDP), it was 4 % (7.3 % between 2000 and 2010); while in the rest of Africa (42 % of African GDP), the growth rate was higher in 2015, at 4.4 % (4.1 % between 2000 and 2010).

But the scenario has been gradually evolving. In Egypt, for instance, the Arab country with the largest population (more than 100m) and with an important strategic position on the Mediterranean Sea, the Suez Canal and access to Sub-Saharan Africa, during the last fiscal year, the rate of growth reached 5.6 %, higher than the 5.3 % growth of the previous year. The ratio of budget deficit to GDP has started to reduce (from 12.2 % in 2015 to 8.2 % in 2018), alongside a similar pattern for the debt ratio, thus contributing to encouraging a flow of foreign investments. But notwithstanding these achievements, the number of Egyptians living below the threshold of poverty ($1.45 per diem) has increased from 27.8 % in 2015 to 32.5 % in 2018.

Generally, following the end of the deep financial crisis, economic recovery in Sub-Saharan Africa is projected to pick up from 3 % in 2018 to 3.5 % in 2019 and 3.7 % in 2020, but differences remain between specific countries. The 21 more diversified economies are expected to grow rapidly, but the other 24 more resource-dependent economies will

---

[6]   Latest figures on African growth can be found in the IMF's *Sub-Saharan Africa Regional Economic Outlook,* published twice a year.

remain at a rather low level in the near term, including Nigeria that has attained a 1.9 % increase in 2018 and is expected to reach 2.1 % in 2020. In the first group of countries, growth has been spurred by higher level of public investment, with a parallel increase in public debt, that will present problems in the future if new fiscal space is not created. In the more resource-intensive countries, a fiscal and external account adjustment to lower commodity prices is urgently needed, since volatility has increased, with another sharp fall in oil prices at the end of 2018.

Non-resource intensive countries are expected to continue growing rapidly at about 6.3 % on average in 2019–2020, with an increase in Ethiopia up to 7.7 %. Growth will continue to be driven not only by high public investment, but also by private consumption, especially in the western and eastern part of the Sub-Saharan region. In the whole area, including more diversified economies and resource-intensive countries, medium-term growth is predicted to reach 3.75 %: while this implies an increase in per capita income up to 1.25 %, this is absolutely inadequate to reach the average standard of living prevailing at the world level and, above all, to help create the number of jobs needed to absorb new entrants to labor markets.

7. Factors Favoring African Growth

Despite the slowdown in growth rates in recent years, the overall outlook remains promising: African GDP is still expanding faster than the world average, and there are certain factors that will significantly contribute to increase the speed of economic growth in African countries. The first is rapid urbanization, strongly correlated to the rate of real GDP growth, as productivity in cities is more than double that in the countryside. Granted, urbanization can breed misery if it creates slums; but in many African countries, urbanization is boosting productivity (which rises as workers move from agricultural work into urban jobs), demand, and investment.[7] Companies achieve greater economies of scale by spreading their fixed costs over a larger customer base, and urbanization is spurring on the construction of more roads, buildings, water systems, and similar projects. Since 2000, Africa's annual private infrastructure

---

[7]   Leke A., Lund S., Roxburg C., and van Wamelen A., *What's Driving Africa's Growth*, Seattle: McKinsey Global Institute, 2010.

investments have rapidly increased; nevertheless, more investment is required if Africa's new megacities are to provide a reasonable quality of life for the continent's increasingly large urban classes.

Africa has a large and young workforce, an important asset in an ageing world. An expanding working-age population is generally associated with strong rates of GDP growth. The employment of this workforce depends largely on the capacity of African countries to fully exploit the huge potential of an accelerating technological change. This in turn is closely linked to a massive increase in expenditures targeted on creating human capital. Furthermore, Africa contains 60 % of the world's unutilized, but potentially available, arable land, as well as the world's largest reserves of mineral resources.

The average fiscal deficit in the region is expected to narrow to about 3.2 % in 2019–2020 and continue a consolidation path beyond 2020. While some countries have made some progress on domestic revenue mobilization, most have not. Weak revenue administration and narrow tax bases continue to hold back domestic revenue mobilization. Overall, for sub-Saharan African countries, the revenue gap is estimated at 3–5 % of GDP, and it is not expected to be closed in the medium term.

8. Factors Restraining African Growth

The exploitation of this growth potential is mainly hampered by the lack of availability of much needed investments in infrastructures. For instance, 600m Africans are without any electricity. The African Union has agreed to create a Continent-wide Agency for electrification, which has drawn up a plan to reach the goal of 100 % electrification in 10 years. The implementation of this plan will require financial aid from the EU of $5bn yearly for 10 years, and this will provide the leverage for releasing the private funds of up to $250bn needed to realize the plan.

Moreover, 300m Africans are without access to clean water, and only 5 % of available arable land is correctly irrigated. But beneath the dry African soil, there are abundant reserves of underground water: according to recent research[8] by the British Geological Survey and

---

[8]   See: MacDonald A.M., Bonsor H.C., O'Dochartaigh B.E., and Taylor R.G., "Quantitative maps of groundwater resources in Africa", *Environmental Research Letters* 7(2). 2012.

the University College of London, these reserves are 100 times greater than the volume of water available above ground. The supply of water could be further increased through the use of the new, technologically advanced, desalination plants. This opportunity could be exploited if the electricity required is provided through major investments in solar energy production.

Climate shocks such as excessive rains or a delayed rainfall season can reduce agricultural output, increase food imports, reduce exports and increase public spending. Below-average precipitation can reduce growth by up to 1.5 % in extreme cases, while weather variable conditions can be a factor favoring conflicts in the region.

The average current account deficit in the balance of payments is expected to widen to 7.3 % of GDP in 2019 from 6.6 % in 2018. These current account imbalances vary widely between countries, with no gap between oil-exporting states to large imbalances in non-resource-intensive and other resource-intensive countries. The amount of foreign exchange reserves remains below levels deemed adequate, being projected to fall to an equivalent of 3.7 months of imports.

9. The African Free Trade Area (AfCFTA)

The African Continental Free Trade Area is a trade agreement between 27 African Union member states, signed in Kigali (Rwanda) on 21 March 2018. Ratification by 22 member states was required for the AfCFTA to enter into force. When the process is completed, the AfCFTA will have built up a market of 1.2bn people with a total GDP of $2.5tn.

The importance of the creation of a continental domestic market cannot be underestimated in view of stimulating a process of endogenous growth within Africa. The domestic market of national States is not large enough to guarantee an outlet for industries of a sufficient size to be competitive in the international market. In the last two decades, intraregional imports have reached a 12–14 % share of total imports, and in this process regional trade hubs have emerged. Great opportunities exist to increase regional trade integration, but poor trade logistics and infrastructure are major obstacles to reach this objective. Bringing the quality of logistics to the average global level, with an improvement of about 19 %, would increase intraregional trade by over 12 %, while approaching the average in infrastructural quality with an improvement of about 40 % would drive a 7 % increase in intraregional trade flows.

According to a recent estimate by the IMF "eliminating tariffs on 90 percent of existing intraregional trade flows would increase regional trade by about 16 percent, or $16 billion over time",[9] but the temporary adverse effects of trade liberalization on income distribution should be faced through income support and training programs. Europe could play a role in providing technical and financial support to ensure improvements in logistics and infrastructure, while financial integration should be supported, promoting *inter alia* the creation of a multicurrency clearing center.

10. The Priorities of a European Social Green New Deal

In the newly elected legislature of the European Parliament, an urgent need to plan an agenda to manage structural intervention, to support the sustainable development of the European economy, is generally recognized as a high priority. This in particular calls for an accurate definition of the goals of a *Social Green New Deal* that now appears to be the center of political debate. In the first place, the problem of curbing CO_2 emissions should be addressed. The 2015 Paris agreements are important, as 195 countries have been involved, committed to implement national programs for limiting a quantity of emissions that is compatible with maintaining an increase of average global temperature well below 2°C. However, these agreements are largely insufficient: national programs are ineffective in reaching the fixed objective, while financial resources are much too restricted.

In Europe, there is a broad consensus on the idea that, in order to fight global warming by limiting the use of greenhouse gases, it is necessary to complement market instruments, like the tradable emission permits, with fiscal measures, in particular with a carbon price fixed according to the carbon content of fossil fuels. This price should be backed by a border tax adjustment on imported goods originating from countries that do not put a price on carbon. This strategy implies that from the outset the carbon price should be high enough to provide a signal to the market that eventually consumers and producers should get rid of the use of

---

[9]   IMF, *Sub-Saharan Africa. Recovery Amid Elevated Uncertainty*, April 2019.

fossil fuels, but also that the price must be raised gradually up to the level fixed *ex ante* as the objective to be reached, so that the adjustments needed following the higher price of energy could be implemented without excessive costs. But, at the same time, with the carbon dividend resulting from fixing a price on carbon two other important goals should be pursued: a guarantee of social equity and the support of an ecological transition.

11. Carbon Dividend and Fiscal Reform

The introduction of carbon pricing should be shaped according to the principle of revenue neutrality, since all receipts should be recycled into the economy, primarily to avoid a negative macroeconomic impact. But other important reforms should be introduced in the European fiscal structure,[10] making use of the carbon dividend (deriving from the price increase of fossil fuels) to reduce taxes on lower incomes, in particular on labor incomes, in order to balance the burden of higher taxation of energy on poorest families and to guarantee the social equity of the move. However, this dividend opportunity should also be exploited to start up a process aimed at the necessary transition of economic structures toward the goal of a carbon-free and highly competitive economy in a globalized market.

This process is challenging and expensive. To reach the goal of sustainable European development – from a social viewpoint as well – tax reductions in favor of families and firms implementing programs promoting energy efficiency (improvements of building structures, exploitation of solar energy and other renewables, sustainable mobility) should be introduced. At the same time, support must be guaranteed for the investments needed for creating adequate infrastructure (cheap and eco-compatible public transport, urban renewal, new localization of productive activities to cut down the costs of movements from home to work) and for funding programs of research and development that will promote the changeover from fossil fuels to renewable energy in a short period of time and with reasonable costs, without impairing the process of growth and the welfare level of the European people.

---

[10] Majocchi A., *A Carbon Dividend and Tax Reform*, Comment n. 148, Centro Studi sul Federalismo, Torino, May 2019.

12. European Budget and Own Resources

Over the last years, two facts have become apparent – firstly, the European budget is too small to face the challenges with which the European Union is confronted. These include: internal and external security; the promotion of a carbon free growth model; investments to promote the transition to a digital economy; supporting the competitiveness of European production through funding basic research, and guaranteeing high employment, mainly to new generations; production of public goods to improve citizens' quality of life – through the needed reforms of the welfare systems following the extension of life expectancy, the structural changes in the labor market and the technological evolution in the health system; financial assistance to competitive SMEs and to innovative start-ups in the sector of leisure time, artistic production and the conservation of natural and cultural resources; adequate funding of a European Stabilization Fund able to face effectively in the future general or asymmetric shocks hitting the Union.

Secondly, if the Union continues its dependency on Member States' contributions for financing the budget, European decisions will be weak and delayed, as was the case during the financial crisis. If the Union intends developing an autonomous policy, established through democratic procedures – that is with a majority vote – in the European Parliament and in the Council, in the interest not only of the European citizens, but also of the world, a system of own resources should be introduced. This needs to be sufficient to fund the investments needed to ensure a socially equitable and economically efficient ecological transition, and to promote the development of countries, in particular on the African Continent; their future growth is essential to the success of a European *Social Green New Deal* and to a progressive resolution of the problem of migration, combining solidarity with a rational management of the inflow of migrants to the European territory.

13. The Links between European and African Growth

The sustainable economic development of the European Union is tightly linked to the growth of the African Continent. In the first place, only the growth of Mediterranean or Sub-Saharan countries could in the medium-long term check the flows of migrants toward Europe. Furthermore, there are important and convergent reasons that justify more intense economic relations across the Mediterranean Sea. Ecological transition implies that new sources of renewable energy should be available in place of fossil fuels, in sufficient quantity and at competitive cost, to avoid a dramatic slowdown of production in the European economy. Consequently, the purchase by European firms and consumers of solar energy produced in the desert could raise net disposable incomes in African countries: the ensuing increase in domestic consumption and investment demand will most probably be largely satisfied through a higher amount of imports coming from European markets.

To achieve these goals, a farsighted European policy is required, that will provide a significant amount of resources to fund the investments needed to build plants in African countries for the production of renewable energy and to support research in new technologies able to guarantee this large-scale production of solar energy at competitive costs in the desert region of the Sahara and neighboring countries. Furthermore, the availability of energy will make it possible to build sea-water desalinization plants, that will favor the progressive transformation – at least partially – of the desert into fertile land. At the same time, African countries should be equipped with the human capital needed to open the way toward an economy where the domestic production structure will guarantee a living standard comparable to that of the developed countries and, progressively, to compete successfully on the world market.

14. An African Growth Plan

Investments in water and energy supply and production of human capital are the first requirements for an effective African growth plan, which the European Fund for Sustainable Development should support to effectively deal with the challenge of managing increasing migratory flows toward European coasts. But this plan must comply with political requirements as well. The first is the establishment of political stability and security conditions in those African countries from where migration flows originate, and this should be a priority task in the prospective already defined by the Global Strategy for the EU[11] conceived by Federica

---

[11]   *Shared Vision, Common Action: A Stronger Europe. A Global Strategy for the European Union's Foreign and Security Policy,* Brussels, 28 June 2016.

Mogherini, the former High Representative of the Union for Foreign Affairs and Security Policy.

To be successful, the growth plan should be designed and implemented at the regional level, supported by a regional institutional agreement similar to the European Coal and Steel Community. A Water and Energy Community could represent the first step in this direction. European financial aid is imperative, but the initiative should remain in the hands of the African countries concerned. As General Marshall said in his famous speech at Harvard University on 5 June 1947, launching his plan for European recovery after World War II, "it would be neither fitting nor efficacious for the American government to undertake to draw up unilaterally a program designed to place Europe on its feet economically. This is a business of the Europeans. The initiative must come from Europe and the program should be a joint one". This advice should be taken into account by the European Union now when promoting the External Investment Plan.

15. A European Agency for Energy and Environment

In Europe, ecological transition should be governed through the creation of a European Agency for Energy and Environment (AEEE). A proportion of the carbon dividend could be targeted at funding the Agency that will manage the flow of investments needed to support the transition to a sustainable economic structure. This will give new impetus to the European economy and, at the same time, to financing the African Growth Plan proposed by the countries of the African Continent, with the backing – technical and scientific, and not only economic – of the European Union through its AEEE. The financial resources for the Agency, that will work mainly for promoting investments, could be provided not only by the carbon dividend, but also by the emission of Green Bonds, guaranteed by the own resources that will flow to the European budget through carbon pricing and by revenues from investments financed by the Agency.

The African Growth Plan thus represents an essential element of a European project of sustainable development. The ecological transition could open the way to the promotion of a new phase of growth for Europe, and the AEEE could play a role similar to that played by NASA in supporting American growth. Technological developments can improve the competitiveness of European products on the global market, while the use of the carbon dividend will guarantee that growth will be achieved with a commensurate reduction of inequalities in income distribution and to a higher social equity. But many political conditions will need to be satisfied to make the accomplishment of this European Social Green New Deal possible.

16. Conclusions

This policy package, firstly, requires new resources in the European budget and, secondly, a strengthened European foreign and defense policy. On these two points, some important remarks were made by Ursula von der Leyen in her Opening Statement in the European Parliament in Strasbourg on 16 July 2019[12]. On the Green New Deal, the new President of the European Commission precisely affirmed: "I want Europe to become the first climate-neutral continent in the world by 2050. A two-step approach is needed to reduce CO_2 emissions by 2030 by 50, if not 55%. I will put forward a Green Deal for Europe in my first 100 days in office. I will put forward the first ever European Climate Law which will set the 2050 target into law. This increase of ambition will need investment on a major scale. Public money will not be enough. I will propose a Sustainable Europe Investment Plan and turn parts of the European Investment Bank into a Climate Bank. Emissions must have a price that changes our behavior. To complement this work, and to ensure our companies can compete on a level-playing field, I will introduce a Carbon Border Tax to avoid carbon leakage".

On the second point, von der Leyen, starting from the recognition that "the world needs more Europe", recognized that "Europe should have a stronger and more united voice in the world, and it needs to act fast. That is why we must have the courage to take foreign policy decisions by qualified majority. And to stand united behind them". And in the field of security, the cornerstone has to be the creation of the European Defense Union.

---

[12]   Opening Statement in the European Parliament Plenary Session by Ursula von der Leyen, Candidate for President of the European Commission, Strasbourg, 16 July 2019.

In parallel to these European developments, new links should be established with Africa, in political and economic terms. The starting point should be the definition – in partnership with the African Union – of a Growth Plan, that will ensure a flow of investment, the creation of human capital, environmental improvements and the production of renewable energy. This Plan will start a new phase of ecologically sustainable and socially equitable growth on the Continent, favorable to European growth as well. In this way, a first step will be taken, not only for the improvement of living conditions of African people – that will endorse a progressive reduction in the number of migrants moving toward Europe – but also for a strengthening of democratic processes and, in parallel, of political institutions, that will ensure a new role for the African Continent in the world politics.

References

European Commission (2016), *Strengthening European Investments for Jobs and Growth. Towards a Second Phase of the European Fund for Strategic Investments and a New European External Investment Plan*, Brussels, COM/2016/0581

Flahaux M. L., and De Haas, H. (2016), *African migration: trends, patterns, drivers'*, in "Comparative Migration Studies", 4, 1. https://doi.org/10.1186/s40878-015-0015-6

IMF (2019), *Sub-Saharan Africa. Recovery Amid Elevated Uncertainty*, International Monetary Fund, April.

Italian Non-Paper (2016), *Migration Compact. Contribution to an EU Strategy for External Action on Migration*, April 2016.

Leke A., Lund S., Roxburg C., and van Wamelen A. (2010), *What's Driving Africa's Growth*, Seattle: McKinsey Global Institute. https://www.mckinsey.com/featured-insights/middle-east-and-africa/whats-driving-africas-growth# (accessed May 18, 2020)

Macdonald, A., Bonsor, H., Ó Dochartaigh, B., and Taylor, R. (2012), *Quantitative maps of groundwater resources in Africa*, in "Environmental Research Letters" 7, 2. 024009. DOI: 10.1088/1748-9326/7/2/024009

Majocchi A. (2019), "A Carbon Dividend and Tax Reform", Comment n. 148, Centro Studi sul Federalismo, Torino, May 2019 at http://www.csfederalismo.it/en/publications/comments/1434-a-carbon-dividend-and-tax-reform

Mallett R. (2018), *Exploring Intra- and Extra-Continental African Migration: Trends, Drivers and Policy Options*, in Carbone G. (ed.), *A Vision of Africa's Future. Mapping Change, Transformations and Trajectories Towards 2030*, Milano: ISPI.

Opening Statement in the European Parliament Plenary Session by Ursula von der Leyen, Candidate for President of the European Commission, Strasbourg, 16 July 2019

Shared Vision, Common Action: *A Stronger Europe. A Global Strategy for the European Union's Foreign and Security Policy*, Brussels, 28 June 2016

The New Africa-Europe Alliance

OLIMPIA FONTANA

1. Synergies of EU – Africa Cooperation

In a rapidly evolving global context, the European Union (EU) is looking more and more closely at relations of mutual cooperation with Africa, with the awareness that the two Continents have much to gain from closer cooperation. A change of pace took place at the Africa–EU Summit in Lisbon with the launch in 2007 of the Joint Africa-EU Strategy (JAES), setting out the intention of both partners to move beyond a donor-recipient relationship toward long-term cooperation on jointly identified, mutual and complementary interests. Although in more than 10 years the Strategy has not produced the expected results, the narrative of wanting to overcome the traditional partnership based on development aid is still vibrant.

In September 2018, the European Commission launched a "New Africa – Europe Alliance", focused on the creation of sustainable investment and jobs (European Commission, 2018).[1] The Alliance is mainly an economic and financial plan that fits into the vision already defined by broader international frameworks, such as the United Nations Agenda 2030 and its 17 Sustainable Development Goals and the 2015 Paris Agreement. At the center of the initiative are the deepening of economic integration and trade relations both within the African continent and with Europe, on one hand, and a comprehensive plan for strategic investments on African ground, on the other. The two initiatives

---

[1] European Commission (2018), *Communication on a new Africa – Europe Alliance for sustainable investment and jobs: taking our partnership for investment and jobs to the next level,* COM(2018) 643.

are closely linked, as investment, especially in infrastructure, is essential to promote economic activity and allow trade, while at the same time investors need a strong positive investment climate, which depends on economic prospects and the existence of product and service markets.

In the JAES, Africa has called for the recognition of a partnership "based on a Euro-African consensus on values, common interests and common strategic objectives", guided by the principle of "interdependence between Africa and Europe, ownership and joint responsibility" of various challenges that both continents are facing. Europe's quest is both for new markets and investment opportunities in which to make use of excess savings that underpin its macroeconomic situation, and for a shared management of the migration issue, in which the Alliance is part of a more comprehensive approach. Africa, conversely, is a fast-growing continent, with a young population, that is taking steps toward greater internal economic integration. Its development must build on the diversification of its economy and investment, new technologies and economic models that can help Africa to embark on a path of sustainable development.

2. African Trade, between "old" and "new friends"

The long-term aim of the EU is to create a comprehensive continent-to-continent free trade agreement with Africa. Although trade relations between the two partners are important, they are still limited and subject to increasing competition from other players, in particular from China. To Europe, Africa is the fourth trading partner, as a continent, with a share of the European international trade of 7,5 % (as an average between import and exports), after Asia (41 %), other European non-EU countries (24 %) and North America (19 %) (Eurostat, 2019).[2] For Africa, the EU remains the largest trading partner: in 2017, 37 % of exports and 35 % of African imports (with a total value of €243bn) were with the EU. At the national level, the main African trade partners are South Africa, Algeria, Morocco and Nigeria, accounting for more than half of total African trade with the EU.

---

[2] Eurostat (2019), *The European Union and the African Union. A statistical portrait*, https://ec.europa.eu/eurostat/documents/3217494/9767596/KS-FQ-19-001-EN-N.pdf/376dc292-0d2d-4c66-9a36-5bc63c87466c.

In terms of products, the EU's major imports from Africa are above all energy products, in particular crude oil, for which Africa is second only to Russia, followed by food and live animals. The main products Africa requires from the EU are machinery and vehicles, in particular motor vehicles. This imbalance in trade flows – raw materials against manufactured goods – places Africa at the bottom of the value chain, with Europe at the top: this nevertheless reflects the production structure of African economies, highly dependent on raw materials.

Europe's trading prominence in the African continent is however being challenged, as there are signs of a change in the relative weight of international trade partners. In recent years, the trend has been toward a decrease in trade relations with Europe, considered the continent's "old friend": trade with new partners has grown, namely the BRICS (Brazil, Russia, India, China, South Africa), and in particular China, which from 2017 has now become the continent's "new friend", just behind the EU, with a total volume of $101bn.[3] Alongside this, trade relations between African countries themselves, considered "good friends" as internal trade is less vulnerable to external shocks, remain stable, albeit at lower levels (Sandrey, 2015).[4]

2.1 Intra-African trade between "good friends"

The African Continental Free Trade Agreement (AfCFTA), signed in March 2018, represents the continent's most ambitious integration initiative. The main objectives are the creation of a single continental market for goods and services, with free movement of business, persons and investments; the expansion of intra-Africa trade across the Regional Economic Communities (RECs) and the continent in general; and the enhancement of competitiveness and support of economic transformation. Intra-African trade is in fact still relatively underdeveloped, accounting for less than 20 % of the continent's total trade. The main actor in intra-African trade is South Africa. For some countries like Morocco, Nigeria

---

[3]   Data from Ministry of Commerce People's Republic of China, at http://english. mofcom.gov.cn/article/statistic/lanmubb/AsiaAfrica/201907/20190702886320. shtml.

[4]   Sandrey R. (2015), *The African trading relationship: new, old and good friends*, Tralac ebook, at https://www.tralac.org/publications/article/8223-africa-s-trade-relations-old-friends-good-friends-and-new-friends.html.

and Egypt, intra-African trade is a small part of their international trade, while for others, like Zimbabwe, Uganda and Tanzania, the share of trade within Africa is about half of their total volume. The agricultural products traded within the continent accounts for 19 %, while the rest is dominated by non-agricultural goods, like mineral fuels, oils and gas, gold and diamonds, all commodities that play an important role in the intra-African trade balance (Tralac, 2019).[5]

One of the reasons for this low level of trade between "good friends", i.e., African countries themselves, is the dependence of domestic economies on the production of raw materials, with a specialization limited to one or a few products. Such a structure does not facilitate internal trade relations, due to a low level of complementarity between economies, and above all does not permit the creation of internal value chains, which would allow greater diversification of production. On the contrary, low diversification exposes domestic economies to the impact of price fluctuations and natural disasters for agricultural products, in particular. Although African countries sees their GDP growing, the effects of fluctuations in world market prices for raw materials and in particular the decline in prices of crude oil and natural gas have curtailed the economic output of a number of countries. Nevertheless, African GDP growth rates in 2017 outstripped the growth rates of the best performing EU countries, with almost 4 % on average for Africa, compared to less than 2 % for EU.

Other obstacles limit the development of intra-African trade. For example, a protectionist trade policy between African countries themselves, in contrast to Europe's greater openness to imports, helps to create an imbalance in external trade relations. A large majority of African countries belong to the World Trade Organization (WTO). Nevertheless, trade policies are, in most cases, protectionist. In most African countries effectively applied tariffs rate are very high, between 17 % and 6 % (Dabrowski and Myachenkova, 2018),[6] not only higher than those applied in the EU and US, but also in developing countries

---

[5]   Tralac (2019), *The African Continental Free Trade Area, a Tralac guide – 5th edition*, at https://www.tralac.org/documents/resources/booklets/2878-afcfta-a-tralac-guide-5th-edition-june-2019/file.html.

[6]   Dabrowski M. and Myachenkova Y. (2018), *Free trade in Africa: An important goal but not easy to achieve*, Bruegel Blog Post, at https://bruegel.org/2018/04/free-trade-in-africa-an-important-goal-but-not-easy-to-achieve/.

like those belonging to the Association of South East Asian Nations (ASEAN-5), their competitors. Even being part of one or more of the eight RECs does not offer many reduced tariff preferences, or indeed an incentive for regional trade, which remains stagnant. Finally, non-tariff barriers also contribute to discrimination against intra-continental trade as compared to trade with external partners, while the free movement of people within the continent is difficult. In this respect, the creation of an African passport, which is fundamental to the free movement of people, is being discussed within the African Union.

2.2 Complementary policies to African integration

An important ingredient in African economic integration is the introduction of a common currency. The Treaty of Abuja establishing the African Economic Community provides for the creation of the African Central Bank by 2025 and a new single currency, the *Afro*, which will be achieved through the creation of regional monetary unions, each with the adoption of different currencies linked to the euro, pound and dollar. Achieving a single African currency would represent an important political result, with the *Afro* becoming a symbol of African unity, as well as producing benefits in terms of greater trade integration. However, an assessment of the costs that would result, such as the loss of states' individual monetary policy to respond to asymmetric shocks, should not be neglected. While monetary unions can deliver low inflation and greater stability in good times, the absence of a nominal exchange rate anchor may mean that African economies are vulnerable to persistent real exchange rate misalignment. That makes it all the more important to focus on issues of fiscal flexibility. A monetary union needs to coordinate the fiscal policies of its member countries; but different countries, with their structural differences, may need different fiscal stabilization at different times. A solution could be a mechanism of transfers to member countries in the event of a negative shock, aiming at supporting employment or investments. However, the experience of the euro itself shows the difficulties in building a stabilization instrument because of the lack of solidarity to assemble fiscal resources.

Economic integration through trade liberalization needs to create complementarities between its member countries and therefore requires measures to correct regional imbalances that may arise. Some limited progress has been made toward creating financial support to compensate for further economic integration. For example, the Economic Community of West African States (ECOWAS), a community with a very wide diversity of economies in terms of size, development and resources, equipped itself with the Bank for Investment and Development (EBID). It operates through two subsidiaries, the European Regional Development Fund (ERDF) and the ECOWAS Regional Investment Bank (ERIB). The ERDF focuses on the public sector, particularly financing basic economic infrastructure and poverty alleviation projects, while the ERIB concentrates on promoting the private sector as an engine of sustainable growth.

The risks to which the most vulnerable economic actors are exposed, such as local manufacturers, need to be balanced with support for the creation of employability, such as technical, entrepreneurial or even simply basic literacy skills: education, training and support for small and micro-enterprises to adapt to new structural market conditions. In Africa, in addition to unemployment, there is a problem of misalignment of skills, known as skills mismatch, i.e., a discrepancy between what is learned at school and what is required in the labor market. Against this trend, the EU has made available in the period 2014–2020 through the Pan-African Program (one of the main EU financial instruments for the implementation of the 2007 Joint Strategy) about €230m, to provide young people with market-oriented skills, modernize higher education, improve mobility within the continent and with Europe, and support technological innovation.[7]

2.3 How to move Africa-Europe integration forward

The long-term perspective within the New Alliance is to create a comprehensive continent-to-continent free trade agreement between the EU and Africa. The Commission intends to exploit to the greatest extent the Economic Partnership Agreements (EPAs) African countries have with the EU. However, this action could have problematic implications in terms of achieving greater intra-African integration through the AfCFTA, to which the EU gives its full support.

---

[7] See the Multi-annual Indicative Programme (MIP) 2014–2017 and 2018–2020, at https://ec.europa.eu/europeaid/regions/africa/continental-cooperation/pan-african-programme_en.

First, the EPAs are negotiated between the EU and five different blocks which, in most cases, do not correspond to the eight existing RECs, recognized as the building blocks of the African Union. Therefore, there is a risk that the provisions of the EPAs will complicate the adoption of Common Internal Tariffs, which in turn is a critical step toward the consolidation of RECs into Custom Unions (Karingi et al., 2015).[8]

Second, the institutional framework, set up under the Cotonou Agreement between the EU and ACP (Africa, Pacific and Caribbean) countries, is complex. The "hybrid solution" proposed by the EU post-Cotonou seeks to frame relations between Africa and the EU through an "African Pillar" within the ACP-EU framework; however, the role of the AU here is unclear. Whereas the ACP is traditionally a tool to facilitate the delivery of traditional Official Development Assistance (ODA), the AU is in reality seeking a partnership relationship with the EU that goes beyond development aid (Medinilla and Bossuyt, 2019).[9] This divergence between institutional actors could lead to solutions of greater or lesser symmetry in future trade relations between the two sides of the Mediterranean.

Third, the impact of the EPAs on intra-regional trade could prove controversial. The gradual opening up of trade from Europe could end up granting more favorable treatment to a number of EU imports, compared to similar African products. Therefore, unless the various RECs decide to reduce their respective tariffs, European products may end up substituting intra-African exports. However, apart from tariffs, numerous non-tariff barriers add to the protective measures that can effectively stop cross-border trade in goods and, especially, in services. The Agreement establishing the AfCFTA also explicitly provides for efforts to progressively eliminate non-tariff barriers to trade.

Trade liberalization, within the RECs, intra-African, and between the EU and Africa, is an essential step for a strong partnership between the two continents, and it should evolve toward a new approach that

---

[8] S. Karingi, S. Mevel, G. Valensisi (2015), "The EPAs and Africa's regional integration", in *Bridges Africa*, Volume 4 – Number 6.

[9] Medinilla A. and Bossuyt J. (2019), *Africa-EU relations and post-Cotonou: african collective action or further fragmentation of partnerships?*, ECDPM Briefing Note 110, at https://ecdpm.org/wp-content/uploads/BN-110-Africa-EU-relations-post-CotonouAfrica-EU-relations-and-post-Cotonou-african-collective-action-fragmentation-partnerships-ECDPM-March-2019.pdf.

apparently is emerging in the New Alliance, at least in its intentions. International trade today has a different meaning than in the past: it is no longer a question of producing something in one country and selling it in another, but rather of cooperating across borders to minimize production costs and extend market coverage (AfDB, 2018, p. 55).[10] The "value chain" model – the series of activities from production to distribution – has taken on a global dimension, in which the intermediate stages can be carried out in different countries. The objective of integration between the two continents should lead to African economies, even the least developed ones, becoming part of the value chains between the two continents, in a view to a relationship of equals, not only inspired by the principle of "trade, not aid", but also of "co-production" and the sharing of resources. This means supporting a model for African countries focused not only on the export of commodities, as is currently the case, but also on their processing on the ground, encouraging technology transfer, which could enable them to align with European quality standards and the creation of regional value chains.

A similar idea is suggested by "La Verticale", aiming at a new economic partnership between Africa and Europe, based on sustainability and solidarity (Ipemed, 2015).[11] With the crisis of multilateralism and the domination on the geopolitical scene of the G2 (United States and China), Europe has an interest in aiming at regional integration with Africa, for reasons of geographic, cultural and linguistic proximity, and for the synergies that could derive from it. On the one side, European countries could find youth, labor force, new markets and investment potential in the South, while on the other side Africa could benefit from technology, institutional stability, modern governance and the provision of infrastructure.

3. Investment in Africa: Financing and Critical Aspects

The creation of new investment is vital for development, and the EU-Africa Alliance strongly relies on private (domestic and foreign)

---

[10] African Development Bank (AfDB) (2018), *African Economic Outlook 2018*.

[11] Ipemed (2015), *La Verticale. Pour un avenir commun*, at http://www.ipemed.coop/adminIpemed/media/fich_ article/1455616432_la-verticale-tome-1-dec2015enbd.pdf.

investment in Africa. However, investment in the continent shows an unpromising picture: since 2009, foreign direct investment (FDI) inflows to Africa account for less than 5 % of the total inflows worldwide (UNCTAD, 2016).[12] Further, they tend to fluctuate year to year, and to be uneven at the regional level, with a few countries, South Africa, Nigeria, Kenya, Egypt and Morocco, attracting more than half of total FDI. Nevertheless, Europe plays a major role in the continent: in cumulative terms, in 2016 European countries held approximately 40 % of FDI stock, although multinational enterprises, in particular from France and United Kingdom, have been divesting because of rising instability in many African countries.

Investment in infrastructure is also fundamental for greater economic integration between countries, but currently infrastructure in transport, water, energy and ICT in Africa is lacking. Recent estimates suggest that the annual financial gap for infrastructure (the difference between the amount needed to develop Africa's infrastructure and the amount actually invested) ranges from $68 to $108bn (AfDB, 2018). Further, financing needs vary by sector, with water facing major challenges with an 81–84 % shortfall in its annual requirement, while the transport gap is relatively negligible (8 %). The lack of infrastructure is a major obstacle to economic development and trade. For example, in the presence of a restrictive visa policy, the development of digital communications could favor distance relationships between people as well as online commerce platforms. However, only one in five Africans has regular access to the internet. Other problems relate to the cost of electricity, which is four times higher than industrial rates elsewhere in the world, or travel times along key export corridors, some two to three times higher than those in Asia (AfDB, 2018).

In 2017, the total financing of infrastructure in Africa amounted to $81.6bn, an increase of 22 % over the previous year, mainly due to higher reported Chinese investments (ICA, 2018).[13] An important role was played by public investments of African governments themselves (42 % of the total), while external financing in 2017 came mainly from China

---

[12]   United Nations Conference on Trade and Development (UNCTAD) (2016), *World Investments Report 2016*.

[13]   Infrastructure Consortium for Africa (ICA) (2018), *Infrastructure Financing Trends in Africa – 2017*, at https://www.icafrica.org/fileadmin/documents/Annual_Reports/IFT2017.pdf.

(23 %), from the multilateral banks for development, such as the African Development Bank, the World Bank and the European Investment Bank (15 %). About 6.5 % (less than $5 bn) of the total came from Europe, both at the EU and member country level. At sector level, transport was the main destination of funds (41 % of the total), in particular from China, that in 2013 announced the construction of the Mombasa-Nairobi railway in Kenya and the railway linking Addis Ababa with Djibouti's port-capital on the Red Sea, followed by the energy (29 %), water (16 %) and ICT (2 %) sectors. Finally, the financing trend by region saw West Africa as the main destination, with increasing financing since 2013 (26 % in 2017), North and East Africa (both 17 %), Southern Africa (excluding Republic of South Africa) (14 %), while Central Africa continues to remain the least attractive for investors (7 %).

In conclusion, closing this gap has for many years been given a high priority in many African countries, whose governments are generally the main contributors to total infrastructure spending. However, foreign investors are needed to meet Africa's substantial investment requirements effectively. Institutional investors such as insurance companies, pension funds, and sovereign wealth funds have more than $100tn in assets under management globally. In perspective, then, a small fraction of the excess global savings and low-yield resources would be enough to plug Africa's financing gap and finance productive and profitable investments. To be sure, however, insufficient stock and poor quality of infrastructure are not just about limited resources, but can also be partly attributed to a shortage of bankable projects and effective institutional arrangements able to attract investors.

3.1 Alternative form of financing: blending finance

Foreign financing of development relies on a variety of sources, both public, such as ODA, and private, such as FDI. For some countries, such external financing is a substantial resource that indicates a strong dependence on foreign aid. As regards the private sector, Africa is only capable of attracting a very small part of total global investment. For some years now, there have been developments in the use of financing resources. The UN 2030 Agenda for Sustainable Development places new emphasis on the blending between traditional ODA or other philanthropic resources that are the tools foreseen by the Millennium Development Goals (MDGs), with other resources of private investment to finance sustainable development, resulting in positive outcomes for both investors and communities. The underpinning rationale is the concept of "additionality" where the blending of public finance leads to an additional result than would not happen otherwise.

Furthermore, the blending of finance encourages an exchange of knowledge between private operators, who have entrepreneurial skills but are not very familiar with the context in which the project is carried out, and public institutions, which can provide the missing information. The reasons for the unattractiveness of investment are many, from structural and institutional flaws, like corruption and the lack of rule of law and independent legislative power; to projects that are insufficiently profitable, despite potentially high economic, environmental and/or social benefits, with excessive risk profiles, or located in already heavily indebted countries, meaning that they have to comply with International Monetary Fund (IMF) requirements for loans.

The EU has pushed the blending agenda in Africa since 2007 as an instrument to support its external policy objectives, through the creation of the EU-Africa Infrastructure Trust Fund (EU-AITF), which became in 2015 the Africa Investment Facility (AfIF), mainly funded by the European Development Fund (EDF). Between 2007 and 2015, total investments of €57bn have been made (€7bn a year), based on a public contribution of €3.4bn in sectors such as energy, transport, water and sanitation, and private sector development. In September 2017, the AfIF was transformed into the Africa Investment Platform (AIP) and became an integral part of the European Fund for Sustainable Development (EFSD), the new EU initiative for investment in Africa and in the neighborhood, also known as the External Investment Plan.

3.2 The EU External Investment Plan

In 2017, the European Commission announced a new European "External Investment Plan" (EIP), aimed at African and neighborhood countries. Its overall aim is to promote sustainable private investments with a view to tackling some of the root causes of migration from Africa and the EU Neighborhood, and more broadly to contribute to sustainable development. The EIP provides for the establishment of the European Fund for Sustainable Development (EFSD). The aim is to address the fragmentation of efforts and approaches that have characterized blending finance so far and provide an integrated framework for development that goes beyond pure investment promotion. An important role is played by "soft infrastructure", i.e., collateral initiatives that range from technical assistance to support for reforms to improve the business environment. For this reason, the EIP includes two other pillars, in addition to the EFSD. One is the technical assistance from financial institutions, such as the EIB, to formulate and publicize attractive projects; the other is the promotion of a more investment friendly policy, regulatory and business environment through dialogue with governments, entrepreneurs and civil society in the beneficiary countries.

With respect to the first pillar, it must be said that EFSD, amounting to €4.1bn, consists of both pre-existing blending facilities (€2.6bn coming from the former AfIF and the Neighbourhood Investment Facility) and a new guarantee instrument of €1.5bn, half of which comes from the Community budget (€350m) and the EDF (€400m), and half are contingent liabilities in case of need (€750m) (European Commission, 2017).[14] By 2020, the EFSD is expected to leverage €44bn of actual investment, which, if national contributions were added, could double. As regards the guarantee, the Commission has allocated the entire amount through four areas of intervention that are predetermined as follows: sustainable energy and connectivity (39 %), financing for small and micro-medium enterprises and agriculture (33 %), digitization (14 %), and sustainable cities (11 %). Most of the EU investment program for Africa is devoted to the production of renewable energy in urban and rural areas and to the support of entrepreneurial activities, in particular very small-scale projects and those in fragile contexts.

3.3 Critical aspects of the EIP

In spite of new names for regional blending facilities, the total allocation of the EFSD consists of resources that are not new, but result from their reclassification, and will be split between Africa and the Neighborhood. In 2017, €5.6bn was approved in blending projects in Africa, mostly in the transport and energy sectors, thus almost in line with what happened before the introduction of the EFSD, with the EU-AITF and AfIF. Effectively, the new element of EFSD is the guarantee component, that shifts the focus toward de-risking instruments, instead of subsidizing

---

[14] European Commission (2017), *Questions and answers about the European External Investment Plan*, at https://europa.eu/rapid/press-release_MEMO-17-3484_en.htm.

interest rates to increase the affordability of loans. It will represent the main tool through which the EU will seek to support investment in the most difficult contexts, such as conflict-affected and least developed countries. In fact, one of the critiques often made of traditional aid is that the allocation of resources is concentrated on middle-income countries and on certain sectors, neglecting the objectives of poverty reduction, and therefore increases disparities between countries. The EFSD guarantee should instead generate investment in rural areas and in small/ micro-businesses.

The investment plan with Africa must not overlook the role played by the informal sector in the region. According to the International Labour Organisation, non-agricultural employment in the informal economy accounts for 66 % of total employment in sub-Saharan Africa and 52 % in North Africa. If the informal sector is recognized as "a vibrant, entrepreneurial part of the economy which can stimulate economic growth and job", which represents the dominant share of many sectors, such as manufacturing and trade, then it should be included in the debate. Sparks and Bannet (2010) suggest stimulating transference into the formal sector by removing barriers to greater participation.[15] For example, they propose literacy and vocational training programs aimed at the informal sector, as well as the provision of special social benefits, such as health care, to the informal sector in return for a small contribution, and to increase the capacity to obtain the funding needed to start up new, or expand existing businesses.

However, the EFSD does not allocate new resources with respect to past needs: the investment gap in Africa, not least in infrastructure, needs huge financial resources that Europe alone cannot furnish. However, a closer partnership with Africa should demand more attention from Europe under the next Multiannual Financial Framework with a substantial increase of available funding for that purpose and in specific sectors, like manufacturing and energy. The partnership could produce strategic benefits at various levels: in terms of new markets for goods, services and capital, in light of the long-term period of stagnation; and provide a source of young, connected and skilled workers, to counter an aging

---

[15] Sparks, D. L., and Barnett, S. T. (2010), *The Informal Sector In Sub-Saharan Africa: Out Of The Shadows To Foster Sustainable Employment And Equity?*, in International Business & Economics Research Journal (IBER), 9(5). https://doi.org/10.19030/iber.v9i5.563

European population. Not least, it could create business opportunities for European companies to assure access to electricity in Africa, while tackling climate change as broadly as possible, as the reduction of European CO_2 emissions alone cannot solve this environmental issue. The ambitious Green New Deal project that the European Commission intends to carry out in the next few years absolutely must contain an African component as an integral part of the challenge to climate change.

Energy is a key vector for development: just think of the potential implications for education that the possibility of moving activities, such as studying, to after dark, thanks to the availability of electric light. At the same time, the demand for energy services in the continent will surge in the coming decades in line with the demographic boom (Sartori and Colantoni, 2019).[16] In this perspective, the development of African countries will require a different approach, in contrast to the "business as usual" scenario. Bold actions in a transformative agenda are necessary to concurrently increase the likelihood of meeting SDGs by 2030 and tackle climate change. Accelerated renewable energy growth, (wind and solar), associated with new development models in African countries are two key policy actions that could bring us all on a pathway toward smart sustainable development within global boundaries (Randers et al. (2018).[17] Unlike the energy model developed in Europe, Africa, with a dispersed rural area and a large informal sector, can be best served by a decentralized approach based on small solar panels and batteries in rural areas and micro-grids in urban areas. In this sense, through the EIP, Europe could support major private investments in solar panel systems, especially in view of the ongoing revolution in reducing costs of renewables, and thus respond to the growing demand for energy.

---

[16]   Sartori N. and Colantoni L. (2019), *Empowering Africa*, in Colantoni L., Montesano G. and Sartori N., Empowering Africa. Access to power in the African continent, Bern, Peter Lang.

[17]   Randers et al. (2018), *Transformation is feasible – How to achieve the Sustainable Development Goals within Planetary Boundaries – A report to the Club of Rome, for its 50 years anniversary,* report to the Club of Rome from Stockholm Resilience Centre and BI Norwegian Business School, at https://www.stockholmresilience.org/downlo ad/18.51d83659166367a9a16353/1539675518425/Report_Achieving%20the%20 Sustainable%20Development%20Goals_WEB.pdf.

3.4. *Migration management in the long-term perspective*

Politically, the EIP is framed as part of the EU's response to the perceived migration crisis and therefore tries to address the root causes of migration through a long-term strategy to contain migratory pressures.[18] Apart from the consideration that the bulk of African migration is within the African continent itself, results in terms of reduced migration may not occur very soon, in light of Africa's ongoing demographic transition. In fact, it has been observed in the literature that once economic growth has been triggered in a country, this can increase pressures to emigrate, defined in the literature as the "migratory hump": the increase in per capita income is accompanied by an increase in the level of education, which, however, does not correspond to immediate adequate employment opportunities in the local context.[19] Migration is only reduced when certain levels of general socioeconomic well-being are reached, which, for the majority of the African sub-Saharan countries, where most of the (above all irregular) migration to Europe originates today, can only take place over decades. Financing investments is a way to create local development and contain migration in the very long term, but it requires a complementary management of migration flows which takes into consideration a foreseeable increase, rather than a reduction, over the next decades. The same demographic projections of Europe and Africa suggest an asymmetry between the two continents, in which migration could play an important role. According to forecasts, by 2100, the African population will reach 4.2bn with an average age of 35 years, while the population in Europe is not destined to change much, remaining around 600m., with a tendency to decrease.

---

[18] The fund is framed as aiming to "address specific socio-economic root causes of migration, including irregular migration, and to contribute to the sustainable reintegration of migrants returning to their countries of origin and to strengthening of transit and host communities" (European Union, 2017, Regulation of the European Parliament and of the Council establishing the European Fund for Sustainable Development (EFSD), the EFSD Guarantee and the EFSD Guarantee Fund. (2016/0281 (COD) PE-CONS 43/17). Brussels.

[19] The development-migration link is complex and suffers from other factors, such as population growth, inequality, the emulation effect, whether or not there are obstacles to migration and credit restrictions (see Angenendt S. et al. (2017), *More Development, More Migration?*, SWP Comment 2017/C 40, at https://www.swp-berlin.org/fileadmin/contents/products/comments/2017C40_adt_etal.pdf).

One of the proposals for the EU multiannual financial framework 2021–2027 is to increase the budget for the EU's external action and bring more flexibility to adjust for emergencies.[20] In this vein, on the basis of a "crisis mode" displayed by EU institutions and member states in tackling the migration question, in 2015 the EU created the EU African Trust Fund that spends mainly on "migration management and control", through the securitization of migration, to the detriment of development and poverty reduction objectives (Barana, 2017).[21] The risk of such management of the "migration crisis" is first to feed the perception of Africa as a source of migrants to Europe, and, as a consequence, to divert funds formerly allocated to European development cooperation, since most of the African Trust Fund's resources come from the European Development Fund.

In this perspective, current EU migration policy, based on the closure of borders and the outsourcing of management in return for economic aid, should seek more coherence with the economic framework set by the EIP, leaving room for measures to increase the potential for legal migration, associated with an idea of mobility within a broad geographical continuity between Africa and Europe. Objective 10.7 of the SDGs aims to "facilitate orderly, safe, regular and responsible migration and mobility of persons, including through the implementation of well-managed and organised migration policies". Examples of this could be Community programs to regularly employ low-skilled workers in Europe, perhaps in the form of seasonal workers, usually employed in the informal sector.

3.5 The presence of the "new friend" China

China's presence in Africa began in the late 1960s, with the Chinese decision to financially support the Tanzanian government's project to build the Tazara railway line between Tanzania and Zambia. Since

---

[20] The proposal of the European Commission for the MFF 2021–2027 foresees a new, broader "Neighbourhood and the world" program that lacks explicit details on how it intends to contribute to the achievement of the UN SDGs (Jones A. et al (2018), *Aiming high or falling short?*, ECDPM Briefing note 104, at https://ecdpm. org/wp-content/uploads/ECDPM-2018-BN-104-Analysis-Proposed-Future-EU-Budget-External-Action.pdf.

[21] Barana L. (2017), *The EU Trust Fund for Africa and the perils of a securitized migration policy*, IAI Commentaries 17, at https://www.iai.it/en/pubblicazioni/eu-trust-fund-africa-and-perils-securitized-migration-policy.

then, China has become a significant foreign provider of finance for major infrastructure projects. Between 2000 and 2014, it provided around $86bn in loans to African countries. This commitment has been strengthened through the periodic Forums on China-Africa Cooperation (FOCAC), with an increase from $6bn per year in the period 2000–2014 to $20bn per year in the current phase. Although China is catching up in accumulating investment into Africa, it must be remembered that these investments are still in their early stages, compared with those accumulated by European countries, that continue to be the largest investor in Africa, not only in terms of stock but even in terms of flow (Garcia-Herrero and Xu, 2019).[22] However, the approach with which China is pursuing its interests in Africa has some interesting implications for Europe.

First, China's BRI-related infrastructure program mainly operates through lending to national governments through project finance, in some cases giving rise to problems of excessive external debt.[23] At the last FOCAC, the Chinese government indicated that of the $60bn promised, a smaller part will be in the form of loans, while on the other hand, financing will increase in the form of donations and loans at preferential rates, showing signs of a correction of the risk of a debt trap. President Xi Jinping has encouraged the participation of Chinese private companies in the financing program, although limited to Chinese capital. However, given the large investment needs and the expected population boom in next decades, China's presence in Africa does not pose a risk of crowding out Europe's initiatives.

Second, the way in which China makes infrastructure investments abroad differs from traditional donors, as China is willing to finance projects in the proximity of rural towns and villages that are generally passed over by development finance. Although this approach has positive effects in terms of reducing inequalities between regions, it can lead to

---

[22] Garcia-Herrero A. and Xu J. (2019), *China's investment in Africa: What the data really says, and the implications for Europe*, Bruegel Blog post, at https://bruegel.org/2019/07/chinas-investment-in-africa-what-the-data-really-says-and-the-implications-for-europe/

[23] The case of Sri Lanka, which formally handed over the port of Hambantota with a 99-year lease in order to repay its debts to China, or Kenya, which similarly guaranteed a mortgage in favor of China on the port facilities of Mombasa in the event of non-payment of the debt, are examples of the risk of losing control of strategic commercial nodes.

negative consequences, such as local corruption or cases of environmental degradation caused by the lack of preliminary analysis of the social and environmental impact of projects (Bluhm R. et al., 2018).[24]

Third, as Chinese investments grow, the stability of the region is also becoming a concern from the Chinese point of view. At FOCAC 2018, a fund was launched to promote cooperation in areas of peace and security, public order and the fight against terrorism. As in the EIP, the question of investment is therefore part of a broad and multidisciplinary strategy, which provides not only mutual economic opportunities, but also the provision of the soft infrastructure necessary to reduce risk and encourage the emergence of more private investment.

Finally, the impact of any external intervention in Africa, whether European or Chinese, should be considered in terms of effective jobs created. Investment by China in Africa is particularly concentrated in transport and energy infrastructure, namely securing access to resources and using China's excess capacity in construction and transportation, two of China's strategic objectives in Africa (Garcia-Herrero and Xu, 2018). In the light of the demographic boom, it is essential that a program of investment in Africa takes job creation into consideration, with higher attention paid to the more labour-intensive sectors, such as manufacturing, which in turn will contribute to making the local economy more diversified and less commodity-dependent.

References (Webpages Accessed before October 2019)

African Development Bank (AfDB) (2018), *African Economic Outlook 2018*, at https://www.afdb.org/fileadmin/uploads/afdb/Documents/Publications/African_Economic_Outlook_2018_-_EN.pdf

Angenendt S. et al. (2017), "More Development, More Migration?", SWP Comment 2017/C 40, at https://www.swp-berlin.org/fileadmin/contents/products/comments/2017C40_adt_etal.pdf

---

[24] Bluhm R. *et al.* (2018), *Connective Financing: Chinese Infrastructure Projects and the Diffusion of Economic Activity in Developing Countries*, Aid Data Working Paper n. 64, at

http://docs.aiddata.org/ad4/pdfs/WPS64_Connective_Financing_Chinese_Infrastructure_Projects_and_the_Diffusion_of_Economic_Activity_in_Developing_Countries.pdf.

Barana L. (2017), "The EU Trust Fund for Africa and the Perils of a Securitized Migration Policy", IAI Commentaries 17, at https://www.iai.it/en/pubblicazioni/eu-trust-fund-africa-and-perils-securitized-migration-policy

Bluhm R. et al. (2018), "Connective Financing: Chinese Infrastructure Projects and the Diffusion of Economic Activity in Developing Countries", Aid Data Working Paper n. 64, at http://docs.aiddata.org/ad4/pdfs/WPS64_Connective_Financing_Chinese_Infrastructure_Projects_and_the_Diffusion_of_Economic_Activity_in_Developing_Countries.pdf

European Commission (2017), *Questions and Answers about the European External Investment Plan*, at https://europa.eu/rapid/press-release_MEMO-17-3484_en.html

European Commission (2018), *Communication on a New Africa – Europe Alliance for Sustainable Investment and Jobs: Taking Our Partnership for Investment and Jobs to the Next Level*, COM(2018) 643, at https://eur-lex.europa.eu/legal-content/EN/TXT/PDF/?uri=CELEX:52018DC0643&from=EN

European Union (2017), *Regulation of the European Parliament and of the Council Establishing the European Fund for Sustainable Development (EFSD), the EFSD Guarantee and the EFSD Guarantee Fund* (2016/0281 (COD) PE-CONS 43/17), Brussels, at https://data.consilium.europa.eu/doc/document/PE-43-2017-INIT/en/pdf

Eurostat (2019), *The European Union and the African Union. A Statistical Portrait*, at https://ec.europa.eu/eurostat/documents/3217494/9767596/KS-FQ-19-001-EN-N.pdf/376dc292-0d2d-4c66-9a36-5bc63c87466c

Dabrowski M., and Myachenkova Y. (2018), "Free Trade in Africa: An Important Goal But Not Easy to Achieve", Bruegel Blog Post, at https://bruegel.org/2018/04/free-trade-in-africa-an-important-goal-but-not-easy-to-achieve/

Data from Ministry of Commerce People's Republic of China (2019), at http://english.mofcom.gov.cn/article/statistic/lanmubb/AsiaAfrica/201907/20190702886320.shtml

Garcia-Herrero A. and Xu J. (2019), "China's Investment in Africa: What the Data Really Says, and the Implications for Europe", Bruegel Blog post, at https://bruegel.org/2019/07/chinas-investment-in-africa-what-the-data-really-says-and-the-implications-for-europe/

Infrastructure Consortium for Africa (ICA) (2018), Infrastructure Financing Trends in Africa – 2017, at https://www.icafrica.org/fileadmin/documents/Annual_Reports/IFT2017.pdf

Ipemed (2015), *La Verticale. Pour un avenir commun*, at http://www.ipemed.coop/adminIpemed/media/fich_article/1455616432_la-verticale-tome-1-dec2015enbd.pdf

Jones A. et al. (2018), *Aiming high or falling short?*, ECDPM Briefing note 104, at https://ecdpm.org/wp-content/uploads/ECDPM-2018-BN-104-Analysis-Proposed-Future-EU-Budget-External-Action.pdf

Karingi S., Mevel S., and Valensisi G. (2015), *The EPAs and Africa's Regional Integration*, in Bridges Africa, Volume 4 – Number 6, at http://www.ictsd.org/bridges-news/bridges-africa/news/the-epas-and-africa's-regional-integration

Medinilla A., and Bossuyt J. (2019), *Africa-EU Relations and Post-Cotonou: African Collective Action or Further Fragmentation of Partnerships?*, ECDPM briefing note 110, at https://ecdpm.org/wp-content/uploads/BN-110-Africa-EU-relations-post-CotonouAfrica-EU-relations-and-post-Cotonou-african-collective-action-fragmentation-partnerships-ECDPM-March-2019.pdf

Pan African Program Multi-annual Indicative Programme (MIP) 2014–2017 at http://news.ucamere.net/Assocamerestero/ACP/SAfrica/DCI%20Pan-African%20MIP%202014-2017.pdf and 2018–2020 at https://ec.europa.eu/international-partnerships/system/files/mip-pan-african-programme-2018-2020-annex_en.pdf

Randers et al. (2018), *Transformation Is Feasible – How to Achieve the Sustainable Development Goals within Planetary Boundaries – A Report to the Club of Rome, for Its 50 Years Anniversary*, Report to the Club of Rome from Stockholm Resilience Centre and BI Norwegian Business School, at https://www.stockholmresilience.org/download/18.51d83659166367a9a16353/1539675518425/Report_Achieving%20the%20Sustainable%20Development%20Goals_WEB.pdf

Sandrey R. (2015), *The African Trading Relationship: New, Old and Good Friends*, Tralac ebook, at https://www.tralac.org/publications/article/8223-africa-s-trade-relations-old-friends-good-friends-and-new-friends.html

Sartori N., and Colantoni L. (2019), *Empowering Africa*, in Colantoni L., Montesano G., and Sartori N. (eds.), *Empowering Africa. Access to Power in the African Continent*, Bern: Peter Lang.

Sparks, D. L., and Barnett, S. T. (2010). *The Informal Sector In Sub-Saharan Africa: Out of the Shadows to Foster Sustainable Employment and Equity?*. In

International Business & Economics Research Journal (IBER), 9(5), at https://doi.org/10.19030/iber.v9i5.563

Tralac (2019), *The African Continental Free Trade Area, a Tralac guide – 5th edition*, at https://www.tralac.org/documents/resources/booklets/2878-afcfta-a-tralac-guide-5th-edition-june-2019/file.html

United Nations Conference on Trade and Development (UNCTAD) (2016), *World Investments* Report 2016, at https://unctad.org/en/PublicationsLibrary/wir2016_en.pdf.

Monetary Aspects of the African Continental Free Trade Area

Elena Flor

The long road to African unity has perhaps taken a major step forward with the decision – adopted on 21 March 2018 and entered into force on 30 May 2019 – by 49 countries to create the African Continental Free Trade Area (AfCFTA), along with the Free Movement Protocol, signed by 32 countries. The AfCFTA is one of the flagship projects of the African Union's Agenda 2063 that also provides for the introduction of a common passport and a single currency.

Established in 1963 as the Organization of African Unity and renamed The African Union in 2002, this organization includes all the countries on the continent and is headquartered in Addis Ababa. So far, the security sector has been its main scope of action with the creation of its "blue helmets", which have intervened on a number of occasions to help stabilize a number of countries troubled by inextricable tribal crises.

The new AfCFTA agreement can provide the same impetus to Africa as the creation of the Common Market did in 1957 to the European unification process.

Reflecting on the African unity issue, the most significant experiences to consider are probably China and India.

China has been able to build on a unification that took place over two thousand years ago, in particular with the concentration of the Seven Kingdoms, and on the creation, under the emperor, of a high-level administrative structure (the mandarins), of which the Chinese Communist Party is, in a way, a continuation. In the last 30 years, the fact that China has again begun to play a key role in the world economy has been facilitated precisely by its historic unification.

In contrast, the Indian Union was the result of the British imperial rule that left local power to the existing dynasties (the Maharajas) and only through Gandhi's action has the current configuration taken shape, by giving an important role to local entities: the Union is divided into 27 states and 16 territories. There are 14 official languages (including English) and only the currency (the rupee) and the army actually are federal competences, while there is still broad autonomy in the field of trade, without even taking into consideration the political structure, in which in many states, alongside the two big federal parties, local political forces prevail.

Based on the Indian experience, strengthening the role of the African Union in the security and monetary sectors is an essential step in the African integration process.

1. The Free Trade Agreement

This agreement, to the extent that it will be implemented, may bring about a decisive turning point in the economy of the African continent.

The economic system of many African states is built on the export of energy resources and raw materials, as well as on the import of consumer goods. Dependence on the prices of raw materials – subject to sharp fluctuations in relation to the evolution of the world economy – and on indebtedness in "hard currencies", explain the recurrent financial crises which have plagued many African countries, forcing them to request IMF support (with the application of the related, conditional, monetary and financial policies) and, in the most dramatic cases, debt restructuring and even cancellation.

The free trade agreement should lead the economy of African states to facilitate import/export with neighboring countries, thus directing imports from developed countries toward investment goods, using investments and aid to build infrastructure capable of breaking down the geographical and technological isolation of individual states.

The first steps in the European integration process after World War II were along these lines, as it was facilitated by the implementation of the Marshall Plan, whose official name was the ERP (European Recovery Program). The first objective was to restore the production capacity destroyed by the war and, not surprisingly, the ERP required a single

European plan that avoided duplication and relaunched trade between European states after the autarky phase.

The implementation of the European Payments Union was at the heart of the ERP, which allowed European countries to balance the settlement of trade between them, without using "hard currency": it was the "dollar shortage" phase. Only the net balance of the European Payments Union had to be settled in dollars, and the Marshall Plan provided that ERP funds could be used for this purpose. The aim was, in fact, to cover European countries' deficit *vis-à-vis* the United States, mainly due to the purchase of capital goods needed for reconstruction.

2. The Monetary Problem in Africa

The need for monetary unification is particularly debated in Africa, which is, in fact, currently organized according to the old colonial areas, with the former French area pegged to the euro, the former British colonies looking for a currency peg and the Mediterranean countries shifting between pegging to the dollar and to the euro.

The African Union, under the 1991 Treaty of Abuja and then the Constitutive Act adopted at Lomé in 2000, decided to create an African Monetary Union, through the integration of the regional monetary zones and based on a single African currency (often named the "Afro"), and the establishment of the African Central Bank (ACB) headquartered in Abuja (Nigeria), the African Investment Bank (AIB) based in Tripoli (Libya) and the African Monetary Fund based in Cameroon.

The process, despite being the subject of continued political meetings and academic debates, will be long (see also the *Annex* for some possible parallelisms with the development of the US Federal Reserve System), but at least it is necessary to identify its direction.

Some steps are essential, especially in the initiation stage of the AfCFTA:

– The implementation, at least between groups of countries with stronger economic and proximity ties that are not part of regional monetary unions, of "payments union" agreements similar to those implemented in Europe after World War II;

– The choice of a "unit of account" as was the case for the European Payments Union, when Robert Triffin created the first "European unit

of account" that, albeit equal to the gold content of one dollar (the famous 35 dollars per ounce) was, after a long journey, to become the euro;
– The choice of a borrowing currency to finance necessary infrastructure capacity that does not undermine African countries' monetary stability due to the monetary policies of the issuing countries.

3. The Special Drawing Rights (SDR) Unit as a Standard for Africa

African countries' choice of the SDR as a "unit of account" may help them meet their needs since:

– it is a more stable "unit of account", especially with reference to the price of raw materials and energy sources;
– it includes the euro and the renminbi, which represent the areas most interested in the development of Africa and its natural resources;
– it may bring the different areas of the continent closer together in relation to their past experiences.

Pegging the potential "Afro" to the SDR "basket" would make the unit of account project more robust, as happened in Europe when the ECU "basket" was chosen to peg the future euro.

The launch, at least between groups of states, of forms of "common agricultural policy" will be necessary to fill the deficit in food production. Europe managed to cover demand in this way, and indeed today is facing the opposite problem: surplus. Agricultural pricing in a "common unit of account" was an essential step and a powerful boost to the next transition to a common currency: the most rational choice would be to use the SDR as the "African agricultural unit of account".

The ACB could indeed perform the significant task – for those countries wishing to participate – of organizing an African Payments Union (APU), in cooperation with the African Export-Import Bank – which is already working on a Pan-African Payment and Settlement Platform. The ACB could, as was the case in Europe, conclude a technical assistance agreement for the functioning of the APU with the Bank for International Settlements (BIS) in Basel. The ACB could also participate in the BIS – as is already the case at present for European countries with the European Central Bank – thus strengthening Africa's role in international monetary cooperation.

African central banks could use the "official" SDRs held – given the lack of international currencies such as the dollar, euro and renminbi – both as capital contributions to the African Central Bank and as capital endowments of the African Investment Bank. In this case, the two institutions could be included in the SDR "Third Party Holders", as provided for in the IMF's Articles of Agreement.

4. The Role of the Mediterranean Countries

It is no coincidence that SDRs, or similar formulas, characterize North African countries bordering the Mediterranean, namely Libya, Egypt and Morocco:

- Libya has formally continued to peg its currency to the SDR, as originally sought by Gaddafi in relation to his "African currency" plan;
- Egypt has continued to determine the Suez Canal tolls in SDRs, which was set at the time of nationalization;
- Morocco has pegged its currency to a basket of euros and dollars (in fact, almost similar to the SDR).

Therefore, an area pegged to the SDR in the Mediterranean area could be developed and, over time, extended to other African countries, with whom economic relations will strengthen.

5. The Banking System's Contribution

The European experience shows how the participation of commercial banks can provide a significant contribution to realizing the monetary unification project, anticipating the creation of a common capital market in the area and encouraging the extended use of the "unit of account" in financial transactions.

In Europe, commercial banks, starting with the *Kredietbank* in Brussels, played a significant role in the use of the ECU unit of account that culminated in the creation of the ECU Banking Association by more than 30 banks, including the European Investment Bank, with numerous ECU-denominated bond issues.

Annex

The Historical Example of the US Federal Reserve System

The Unites States could rely on a Central Bank, albeit intermittently, in the Union's early years. In 1791, the National Bank (namely the "First Bank of the United States") was established, championed by the first Secretary of the Treasury, Alexander Hamilton. It had a 20-year charter which was not renewed by the Congress on its expiration in 1811.

The "Second Bank of the United States" was established in 1816, again with a 20-year charter, which expired – and was not renewed – in 1836. In 1841, the third attempt to establish a national bank failed due to President Tyler's veto.

The monetary unification process could only start again many years later, in 1913, with the enactment of the Federal Reserve Act, following the banking crisis that erupted in California. However, it should be stressed that the aim of the Federal Act was the establishment of several Federal Reserve Banks – no less than 8, no more than 12, again granted a 20-year charter – covering different areas of the country, whereas the Federal Reserve would only act as supervisor: banknotes were to be issued by the Reserve Banks, which were also entitled to set the interest rate of open market operations.

With the Great Depression, the renewal of the 20-year charter was facilitated, while the Federal Reserve powers grew stronger.

It was of utmost importance, however, that from the outset the US could rely on an account unit, the dollar, linked to gold – and to silver as well, in the early stages, according to the principle of "bimetallism".

The introduction of the Afro linked to the SDR is therefore the first necessary step toward the African monetary unification. The second step will be the development of regional central banks, anchored to a common account unit and coordinated by the African Central Bank, as provided by Constitutive Act approved in Lomé in the year 2000.

Contributors

Romano Prodi

President of the European Commission (from 1999 to 2004) and twice Prime Minister of Italy (May 1996 – October 1998; May 2006 – May 2008). President of the African Union-United Nations Peacekeeping Panel (September 2008 – January 2014) and United Nations Special Envoy for the Sahel (September 2012 – January 2014).

Andrea Cofelice

Research Fellow at Centro Studi sul Federalismo.

Giovanni Finizio

Assistant Professor of History of International Relations at the University of Turin and Adjunct Professor at the Universidad Nacional de Tres de Febrero, Buenos Aires.

Elena Flor

Head of Corporate Social Responsibility at Intesa Sanpaolo Bank, Secretary General of Robert Triffin International.

Olimpia Fontana

Research Fellow at Centro Studi sul Federalismo.

Alberto Majocchi

Emeritus Professor of Finance at the University of Pavia, Vice President of the Centro Studi sul Federalismo.

Paolo Sannella

Former Ambassador of Italy to Angola and to the Ivory Coast, President of Centro Relazioni con l'Africa – Società Geografica Italiana.

Federalism

The book series Federalism, run by the Centro Studi sul Federalismo (CSF) aims to disseminate knowledge in the field of studies on federalism, as well as to feed the academic and public debate and support the activity of decision-makers, confronted with demands for autonomy by local governments, along with forms of regional and world integration needed to govern global processes.

The book series is divided into two sub-series: Studies and Classics. The former mostly contains the research outcome and the proceedings of conferences and seminars promoted by the CSF while the latter consists in reprints of the federalist classic works and English translations of Italian federalists' works.

The CSF is a think tank that carries out activities of interdisciplinary research, documentation, information regarding domestic and supranational federalism, developments in the area of regional and continental integration – first and foremost the European Union – and problems related to the world order and the process of democratisation of the international system. The CSF has been founded under the auspices of the Compagnia di San Paolo and the Universities of Turin, Pavia and Milan and has the Turin Polytechnic as co-founder.

Centro Studi sul Federalismo
Piazza Vincenzo Arbarello 8
10122 Torino – Italy
Tel. + 39 011.6705024 Fax + 39 011.6705081
E-mail: info@csfederalismo.it
Website: www.csfederalismo.it

Series Editor: Lucio Levi , Former Professor of Political Science and Comparative Politics at the Turin University, Editor of The Federalist Debate and Scientific Director of the International Democracy Watch

Editorial Board

Paola Bilancia, University of Milan, Board of the CSF

Brendan Donnelly, Director of The Federal Trust, London

Michel Dumoulin, Université Catholique de Louvain

Lucio Levi, University of Turin

Jean-Victor Louis, Université libre de Bruxelles - ULB

Alberto Majocchi, University of Pavia, Vice-President of the CSF

Yves Mény, Luiss School of Government - Rome

Umberto Morelli, University of Turin

Antonio Padoa-Schioppa, University of Milan

José Paradiso, National University of Tres de Febrero - Buenos Aires

Sergio Pistone, University of Turin

Daniela Preda, University of Genoa

Dario Velo, University of Pavia.

Series titles

www.peterlang.com

www.ingramcontent.com/pod-product-compliance
Lightning Source LLC
Chambersburg PA
CBHW050616280326
41932CB00016B/3069